The Abbey of St.Gall
The Ancient Ecclesiastical Precinct

Bernhard Anderes

Translation:
Erika Drucker

1990
First published in German 1987

Suggestions and specialized advice by:

Dr. Ernst Alther, Robert Bamert, Dr. Silvio Bucher, Prof. Dr. Johannes Duft, Dr. Josef Grünenfelder, Markus Kaiser, Dr. Ingeborg Krummer-Schroth, Dr. Michel Reistle, PD Dr. Peter Ochsenbein, Dean Paul Schneider, Dr. Werner Vogler, Josef Wirth.
Proofread by Dr. David Hove.

Illustrations:

Bernhard Anderes, Rapperswil, 62, 64, 68, 70, 83, 89, 98. – Archiv der Kunstdenkmäler des Kantons St.Gallen 15 (Theodor Seeger), 38 (E. L. Noack), 54 on the left (Erwin Poeschel), 69 (Albert Bayer), 105 (Walter Fietz). – Augsburg, Städtische Kunstsammlungen 14. – Freiburg i. Br., Augustinermuseum 22. – Karl Künzler, St.Gallen 6, 30, 102, 103. – Pius Rast, St.Gallen 85, 96, 101. – Foto Zumbühl, St.Gallen 32, 49, 74, 97. – St.Gallen, Kantonsbibliothek Vadiana 10. – St.Gallen, Staatsarchiv 90, 104, p. 214 (on the right), p. 215. – St.Gallen, Stiftsbibliothek 66. – Zürich, Schweizerisches Landesmuseum 3. – Zürich, Zentralbibliothek, Graphische Sammlung 2, 20, 9, 77. – Aerial photograph on cover by Aerobild, Bazenheid.
All unlisted illustrations are from Foto Lautenschlager AG, St.Gallen.
Maps and drawings: Archiv der Kunstdenkmäler des Kantons St.Gallen 17, 34. – Bern, Eidg. Vermessungsdirektion 1 (Permission to reproduce 21. 10. 1987). – Fritz Brunner, Zürich 212, 213. – Gerhard Kasper, Wil, 41. – Repros 18, 51, 52. – Eva Simek, Hochbauamt St.Gallen 65, 93.

① The numbers in the margins refer to the illustrations.

Editor:
Amt für Kulturpflege des Kantons St.Gallen

Distribution:
Buchhandlung am Rösslitor, Webergasse 5, CH-9000 St.Gallen

Printing and design:
U. Cavelti AG, CH-9202 Gossau

Copyright:
Amt für Kulturpflege

ISBN 3-908048-13-3

Contents

Preface

The ecclesiastical precinct of St.Gall was included in the World Cultural Property List by the competent UNESCO committee, meeting in Florence in December 1983, together with the Convent of Muestair and the Old Town of Bern. This great honour brings with it responsibilities which we and the co-proprietors of this centre of culture accept gladly. Among these responsibilities is that of providing appropriate information about the treasures entrusted to us. However, although we have excellent first-hand literature on parts of the ecclesiastical precinct, for example on the Cathedral and the Library, there is no description of the monastery as a whole. It is the aim of the present publication to remedy this lack. We would like to provide the visitor, be he a specialist or not, with an intelligible introduction to a tour of the precinct which should answer any questions he may have during his visit. However, we know that such an array of cultural treasures cannot be absorbed and digested at one go, and for this reason it has also been our aim to give this small book the role of a short reference work. Many of our visitors will appreciate, apart from the text, the numerous illustrations, some of which are little known. One last point: the compact format of this book should make it easy for the visitor to handle.

The Reformed church of St.Laurence, which is situated beyond the limits of the precinct proper, is also described and illustrated. An annotated map provides some brief information on neighbouring architectural monuments and leads on to a walk through the impressive and well-tended Old Town, which it was unfortunately not possible to include in this book.

We would like to thank all those involved in the production of this book, in particular the author, Dr. Bernhard Anderes, the photographers Otmar and René Lautenschlager, and the printing firm of U. Cavelti AG, in Gossau.

We hope that it will help to increase awareness of an item of world cultural property which, in its architectural harmony, its religious art treasures, its archives and library collections, is almost without equal.

Councillor Alex Oberholzer
Director, Department of Internal
Affairs of the Canton of St.Gall

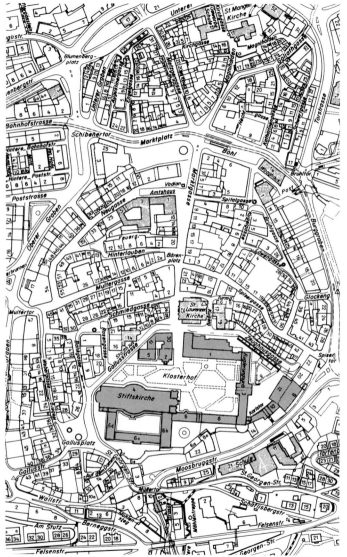

1 The Old Town of St.Gall with ecclesiastical precinct. Scale 1:400.

6

Description

The ecclesiastical precinct of St.Gall is the unique architectural embodiment of 1,200 years of history. In the grounds of the abbey, founded in the 8th century, there rises a monastic town which was conceived anew in the late Middle Ages, took on the shape of a fortified island within the secular town of St.Gall after the Reformation, and finally became a princely residence with a great abbey church during the Late Baroque period. After the dissolution of the monastery in 1805, the newly-formed government of the Canton of St.Gall undertook, together with the Catholic Administration, to maintain and expand the monastery complex, in particular by reconstructing the north side, which served as an arsenal, and the Kinderkapelle (Children's Chapel), and its annexes, on the basis of Baroque construction plans. Almost all the important architectural styles are represented: early Medieval (Carolingian capitals), Gothic (ground plan of the old monastery), Renaissance (the Charles Borromeo Gate with its great sandstone coat of arms), Baroque (the Abbey Church, Library and new Palace), Historicism (the arsenal, Children's Chapel, Great Council Chamber). The monastic complex, which presents a remarkably uniform appearance despite the variety of its architectural periods, is bordered on the north and west by the largely intact medieval town of St.Gall, including the church of St.Laurence and the Gallusplatz (Gallus Square), all of which have been restored very recently.

The Baroque Library is the most beautiful example of this architectural style in Switzerland, and the Cathedral is one of the last great Baroque monastic buildings in the West. With the powerful twin-towered facade of the cathedral and the horseshoe-shaped enclosure, the monastery square possesses a clear, restrained spaciousness.

In addition to this architectural ensemble, priceless cultural treasures have been preserved, in particular the manuscripts and incunabula in the Library, the documents in the Abbey Archives (which are important for the early history of the Alemannian region), the St.Gall State Archives and the Administration Library. Of European significance are the Irish manuscripts, especially those dating back to the 8th and 9th centuries, the illuminated manuscripts of the St.Gall school of painting of the 9th to 11th centuries, and the Carolingian monastery plan of 820–830.

2 The town of St.Gall from the west, with the Gothic church, about 1545. Woodcut by Heinrich Vogtherr. Zentralbibliothek Zurich.

Urban Position

St.Gall is situated in a rather high, narrow valley, which neither climate, commercial circumstances nor geography seem to have predestined to become the site of a prosperous town. More than for any other Swiss town, the monastery was the germ cell that determined the development of the future town. The fortification of the monastery and of the unenclosed settlement by circular walls in the second half of the 10th century provided what was needed for St.Gall to grow into a town, but it only began to develop some 150 years later, when market privileges were granted it (according to Vadian, 1117). Without wishing to go into too great detail we would like to mention a few special features of the ground plan of the old town.

To begin with, there is the raised position of the monastery along the southern slope, where the Steinach stream plunged down and turning sharply to the east, formed a natural trench, which is today covered over by Moosbruggstrasse. Water and water power (mills) were thus very close at hand. Any expansion had to take place towards the north, if the valley was to be a potential commercial axis. The striking position of the monastery on the outskirts of the town was to be advantageous, since the monastery remained an independent structure and provided a rapid connection with the nearby monastic lands. This separate life is still reflected today in the architectural and spatial relationship of the monastery to the town. The church and ecclesiastical buildings lie like immovable blocks scattered in a field of orderly stone. The reformed town and the monastery were separated by walls from 1566 until the 19th century. The Baroque cathedral also gives the town the «cold shoulder», turning its tower-crowned head away from the town and seeming to bow towards the monastic palace. The ground plan mirrors two worlds – that of ecclesiastical absolutism and that of the developed order of the town community: the power of God and the mercy of the Emperor on the one hand, and civic self-awareness on the other.

A·DAS·RATHVS	N·SPISE·RDAR·
B·S·LORENT3M	O·BRVL·DAR·
C·DAS·MVNSTER	P·BLATE·DAR·
D·S·MANGEN	Q·SCHIBEN·DAR·
E·S·KATHRINA	R·MVOLT·ERDAR·
F·DER·SPITAL	S·MVL·ERDAR·
G·DIE·METSE	T·DES·ABTS·DAR·
H·DAS·KARNHVS	V·GRVN·DVRN·
I·BVRGER·MANG	W·LADE·RA·DVRN
K·DAS·IVTHVS	Ÿ·MICHAELS·DV
L·DIE·WAG	J·SCHV·HVS
M·STATAR	X·KIRCH·HAF·

3 The ecclesiastical precinct with partition wall (right) and Charles Borromeo Gate (below). Section from the so-called plan-prospect (a perspective from the air based on measurements taken on the ground) by Melchior Frank, 1596.

Chronology

612   The wandering Irish monk Gallus (died approximately 645) leaves Abbot Columban and establishes a cell and a prayer-house in the Steinach valley.

719   Otmar, the Alemann, takes on the leadership of the brotherhood as first abbot of St.Gall. In 747 he introduces the Benedictine rule and dies in 759 in exile on the island of Werd near Stein am Rhein.

867   The bones of Otmar, who was proclaimed a saint in 864, are transferred to St.Gall.

9th/10th century   Spiritual peak: St.Gall becomes a centre of Western science and culture. The celebrated scriptorium is established. Renovation of the monastery under Abbot Gozbert (ruled 816–837), on the basis of the Carolingian monastic plan still preserved in the Library.

11th/12th century   St.Gall takes the side of the emperor in the investiture quarrel. The assets of the monastery increase but monastic discipline slackens.

13th/14th century   The abbots become involved in state politics. Conflicts with King Rudolf of Habsburg and the Counts of Toggenburg. Internal disintegration. Rise of the town of St.Gall.

Beginning of 15th century   Wars of Appenzell. The monastery loses the lands along the Saentis.

1451   Abbot Kaspar von Breitenlandenberg (ruled 1442–1457) signs a civil law and common law agreement with the confed-

	erations of Zurich, Lucerne, Schwyz and Glarus.
1468	Abbot Ulrich Roesch (ruled 1463–1491) buys the Toggenburg, establishes a territorial state of St.Gall and obtains the title of Prince. Extensive building work at the monastery and on the ecclesiastical lands. Roesch can be considered to be the second founder of the monastery.
1529	Under Vadian, the Reformation gains the upper hand in the town. Destruction of images in the monastery and flight of the monastic community.
1532	After the victory of the Catholics at Kappel, Diethelm Blarer (ruled 1530–1564) is reinstated as abbot and reigning prince. Construction of the first library in 1551.
1555	The monastery of St.Johann in the Thurtal is annexed to the St.Gall monastery.
1556/67	The monastery and the town have sharply separated legal and property regimes. The ecclesiastical precinct acquires its own circular wall and its own gate, the Charles Borromeo Gate.
17th century	The inner life of the monastery experiences a new awakening. Intense building activity: Otmar church 1623, palace wing 1666/67, eastern cloister wing 1674 and numerous additional buildings.
1712	The abbey is occupied by troops from Bern and Zurich. Abbot Leodegar Buergisser (ruled 1696–1717) and the members of the chapter are exiled until the peace of Baden in 1718.
From 1755	Reconstruction of the abbey church and of the library under Abbot Coelestin Gug-

	ger von Staudach (1740–1767). High point of the monastery's splendour.
From 1767	Construction of the New Palace (Pfalz) under Abbot Beda Angehrn (ruled 1767–1796). Construction of numerous new parish churches on the ecclesiastical lands.
1798	The Helvetians put an end to the territorial reign of the abbot and initiate the death throes of the monastery.
1803	Establishment of the Canton of St.Gall. The administration is installed in the new palace (Pfalz).
1805	Dissolution of the monastery of St.Gall by the Great Council (parliament).
1808/10	Modification of the west choir and construction of the high altar in the former abbey church.
1809/13	A Catholic secondary school is established within the former monastery complex. The administration of the church property is entrusted to the Catholic Administration Council as assignee of the abbey.
1824	Establishment of the joint diocese of Chur and St.Gall. The former abbey church becomes a cathedral.
1838/44	The arsenal, the Catholic School and the Children's Chapel are built along the north side of the monastery square.
1847	St.Gall becomes an independent diocese. The bishop takes up residence in the western part of the palace wing, i. e. in the old residence of the abbot.
1866/67	The interior of the cathedral is renovated and receives a new coat of colour.
1881/82	The Throne Room in the New Palace (Pfalz) is transformed into the Great Council Chamber.

1928/36	Extensive external renovation of the cathedral and partial renewal of the sandstone sculptures.
1961/67	Extensive internal restoration and strengthening of the vaulting under the direction of Hans Burkard and Willi Schregenberger, both of St.Gall. The state expert is Albert Knoepfli of Aadorf. Excavation work is carried out by Benedikt Frei of Mels, and Hans Rudolf Sennhauser of Zurzach.
1975/79	Restoration of the exterior and completion of the interior of the arsenal wing. The Abbey Archives, State Archives and the Cantonal Administration Library, as well as the Cantonal Tribunal and other administrative departments are housed here.
1980/81	Restoration of the Great Council Chamber (Historicism style).
1981	Opening of the Lapidarium (stonework museum) in the west vault of the old monastery building.
1989	Restoration of the Baroque facades on the side facing the square.

Stages of Construction

Early and High Middle Ages

The hermitage established by Gallus in about 612 in the Steinach Valley consisted of a small wooden oratory and dwellings for the brothers. St.Gallus' cell was preserved after his death. In 719 Otmar the Alemann founded a proper monastery and built a stone church in the area where the cathedral choir stands now. In 830, Abbot Gozbert (ruled 816–837) laid the foundation stone for a monumental new building, which was consecrated in 839. The excavations carried out in 1964–65 revealed that this church, with its three bays, was based on the Carolingian monastery plan sent by Abbot Heito (d. 836) from Reichenau to St.Gall. It is still kept today in the Library, the most precious building plan dating from the ④ early Middle Ages. However, it would seem that only the eastern sections were built according to this ideal plan, whereas the western sections, with the «Helmhaus» (burial site), the chapel of St.Michael and the church of Otmar, consecrated in 867, were an independent group of buildings which were only annexed in the 18th century, at the time of the reconstruction of the abbey church. To the period before the end of the millennium belong the Otmar crypt built before 980, which still exists, and the Carolingian capitals (today in the Lapidarium, see pp.122ff.). After the invasion of the Hungarians in 926, there was a need for greater security. First, however, the damage caused by an outbreak of fire in 937 had to be made good. In 954, Abbot Anno began to build a circular wall enclosing the monastery and the sparsely settled northern tracts of land, approximately in the region of the later Upper Town. This work was completed by Abbot Notker (971–975). The 10th century saw further ecclesiastical construction outside the monastery proper

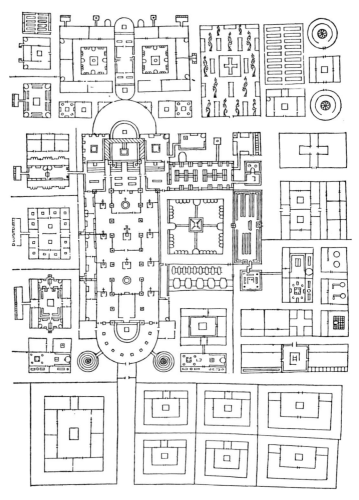

4 Plan of the monastery of St.Gall, about 820/30. Copy, redrawn to facilitate reading of the Carolingian parchment document in the Library of St.Gall: double-choir church with numerous altars and a pair of round towers; right, adjoining cloister with cloister-walk, above novitiate and cemetery, left, abbot's house, school and guesthouse, below and on the right, agricultural buildings.

which has only partially been located, including a Heilig-grabkapelle (Chapel of the Holy Tomb) to the east of the church, a chapel of St.John with a hermitage, a chapel of Saint Catherine containing the tomb of the monk Tuoti-lo, venerated as a saint, and a chapel dedicated to the Holy Cross and Gallus. Further chapels were added later. The fires in the town in 1314 and 1418 also damaged the monastery, but the repairs scarcely altered the old structure. From the early 13th century there existed, outside the enclosure, housing for lay monks, who lived there as canons. Up until that time only the abbot had had an external residence, the palace, which stood approximately in the centre of the present-day monastery square.

Late Middle Ages

With the accession of Abbot Ulrich Roesch (ruled 1463–1491), the building development of the monastery entered a new phase. He not only reorganized the monastery lands and the community, but also proved to be a masterly builder. The choir had been particularly badly damaged by the fire of 1418; the reconstruction, which had soon come to a standstill, was vigorously completed, first by the master of the works HEINRICH GRIFFEN-BERG of Constance, then under KONRAD SCHRADI of St.Gall, and was consecrated in 1483. It was a triple-naved hall with reticulated rib vaulting. The best artists were employed to decorate it, including the fresco painter HANS HAGGENBERG of Winterthur and the cabinet maker HANS OWILER (choir stalls). Abbot Ulrich introduced a great many innovations inside and outside the enclosure, particularly in the cloister. In 1487 he began to build the new monastery of *Mariaberg in Rorschach* and, starting in 1478, the parish church of St.Nikolaus in Wil, which had been annexed to the monastery, was also under construction. The «monastery break» of Maria-berg in 1489, during which the town of St.Gall forestalled by force the dissolution of the monastery, quenched the eagerness to build of the mother monastery, and it was not rekindled, even under Abbot Ulrich's successors, up to the time of the Reformation.

On 23 February 1529 all the altar fittings in the abbey church and in the chapel wcrc destroyed by *iconoclasts.* After the restitution of the monastery in 1532 the chief concern was to make good the damage which had been done and to restore the church fittings. Diethelm Blarer (ruled 1530–1564) was the first abbot to give up the palace as the residence of the prince-abbot. He moved into a wing he had built onto the palace in the northeastern ⑦ corner of the monastery square near the choir of the abbey church. With the construction of a *library,* which was installed in the west wing in 1551, that is, on the same site as the present library, the precious library holdings finally found a permanent home. Abbot Otmar Kunz (ruled 1564–1577) continued the construction of the secular buildings. In 1566, with assistance from the town, he was ③ responsible for the construction of a northern *partition wall.* It was a visible expression of the monastery's separation from the town, a Catholic enclave in the Reformed town. He stipulated that a southern portal be fashioned in the medieval circular wall, so as to provide an approach to the monastery area independent of the town. This is the ⑩⑥ *Charles Borromeo Gate,* through which the saint is said to have been the first to step on his visit to St.Gall on 26 August 1570. At the same time, a new lodging for the brothers was erected along the partition wall, in the area of the present-day Frauenarbeitsschule (Women's Vocational School). CASPAR LINDENMANN, a celebrated sculptor, was responsible for both constructions.

17th Century

After the internal revival of the monastery, Abbots Bernhard Mueller (ruled 1594–1630) and Gallus Alt (ruled

18

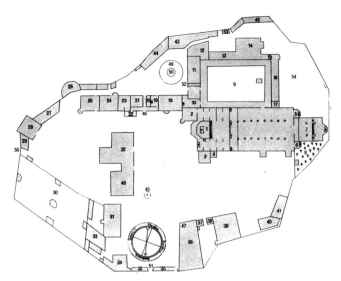

5 *Position of the monastery buildings before the new constructions of the Late Baroque period, drawing following the original of Father Gabriel Hecht, 1719. – 1. The abbey church of St.Gall. – 2. The sacristy. – 3. The choir. – 4. The Mount of Olives. – 5. The Chapel of St.Peter. – 6. The chapel of St.Catherine. – 7. The church of St.Otmar. – 8. The cemetery of the brothers. – 9. The abbey garden. – 10. The chapter hall. – 11. The refectory and three dormitories. – 12. The kitchen. – 13. The museum. – 14. The infirmary and the schools. – 15. The brothers' refectory. – 16. The library. – 17. The archives. – 18. The larder, the abbott's offices and residence. – 19. The Chapel of St.Gall. – 20. The porter's lodgings. – 21. The accommodations for the grooms, the prefecture and the dining-room for guests. – 22. The small room of the porter. – 23. The guests' kitchen. – 24. The bakery. – 25. The pharmacy. – 26. The wheat stores and the arsenal. – 27. The back coach house. – 28. The Charles Borromeo Gate. – 29. The forge. – 30. The garden of the prince-abbot. – 31. The winehouse. – 32. The front coach house. – 33. The cooper's house. – 34. The accommodation for the maids or the school. – 35. The spice stores. – 36. The stables. – 37. The book-binding workshop. – 38. The barber's house. – 39. The brothers' house. – 40. The laundry. – 41. The butchery. – 42. The workshops. – 43. The study hall and the dormitories of the brothers. – 44. The study house. – 45. The courtyard fountain. – 46. The courtyard gate. – 47. The physician's office. – 48. The palace («Pfalz»). – 49. The round garden of the monastery. – 50. The stone fish pond. – 51. The gate to the town. – 52. The gate of the cloister, the deanery and the sub-priory. – 53. The covered fish pond. – 54. The recreation garden. – 55. The small monastery gate.*

1654–1687) came forward as great builders. The western part of the abbey church, which had long been deconsecrated, was demolished in 1623. The Gallus church was extended by approximately one half its length towards the west and in this new construction a new triple-naved church was built in honour of Saint Otmar, the so-called *Otmar church,* which was completed in 1628. Below the west choir still lay the early medieval *Otmar crypt.* The builder of the Otmar church was the Mesoccan PIETRO ANDREOTA of Roveredo. To complete the high altar well-known artists were employed, who were also engaged in artistic production in the lands belonging to the ecclesiastical foundation: the altar builder HANS JOERG DOERIG of Wil, the sculptor HANS SCHENCK of Constance and the panel painter DIETRICH MEUSS of Feldkirch. As early as 1619, Abbot Bernhard had planned to

6 *«Plan prospect» (a perspective from the air based on measurements taken on the ground) of the monastery site from the north. Copper engraving after Gabriel Hecht, 1702.*

7 The New Palace, built 1767/69. Engraving by H. C. Mayr, about 1790. The «Weinschenkenhaus» (wine house) was still standing on the site of the later north wing.

rebuild the monastery; this plan was carried out by Abbot Gallus. The accommodations built by Abbot Diethelm underwent extensive expansion to the east to become the «newe Hofhaltung». This «new court» is the existing wing with the small turret on the square. The two Mesoccan builders GIOVANNI SERRO and GIULIO BARBIERI were responsible for the design and the work was carried out by DANIEL GLATTBURGER, who in 1674 also rebuilt the east wing containing the monks' cells and the refectory. In the late 17th century additional agricultural and out-buildings were erected, of which the so-called winehouse next to the gate opening towards the city remained standing until the 19th century, but was sacrificed for the construction of the arsenal wing.

18th Century

The 18th century did not begin well. Political and religious differences in the Toggenburg led to a dramatic up-

8 View of the monastery precinct from the south, 1986. The main changes have taken place in the south section of the city.

surge in the *War of 1712*. The abbot and members of the chapter fled into exile in Neuravensburg. The monastery buildings and the library were occupied by troops from Zurich and Bern, who did not always take good care of them. The monastery community only returned after peace was signed with Baden in 1718, but the monastery then recovered very quickly. As early as the 1720s there were thoughts of reconstructing the church and monastery, as is shown in early plans by Brother CASPAR MOOSBRUGGER and Father GABRIEL HECHT of about 1721/26, as well as those by JOHANN MICHAEL BEER VON BLEICHTEN of 1730. In 1749 it was decided to rebuild the church, and Abbot Coelestin Gugger von Staudach (ruled 1740–1767) carried the plans forward. In

1750, JOHANN CASPAR BAGNATO submitted a project for future construction, which Brother GABRIEL LOSER transformed into a *model* which still exists. The final construction plans were submitted by PETER THUMB, who built the *nave* and the *rotunda* in 1755–60. Overcoming the initial resistance of the monastic community, Abbot Coelestin also succeeded in having the tower demolished and the *choir rebuilt,* the latter work being carried out in 1761–64 by JOHANN MICHAEL BEER VON BILDSTEIN, with his nephew JOHANN FERDINAND BEER as foreman. The year 1766 also saw the completion of the *twin towers* by the same builders. The decoration, which went on into the 1780s, involved a whole multitude of artists, above all CHRISTIAN WENZINGER, general contractor and sculptor, who was responsible for the overall decoration of the nave and rotunda, the painter JOSEF WANNENMACHER (ceiling paintings), the stucco workers JOHANN GEORG and MATHIAS GIGL (choir), FIDEL SPORER (rotunda altars), FRANZ ANTON DIRR (chancel) and JOSEF ANTON FEUCHTMAYER (confessionals, choir stalls).

9 *Same view of the monastery, with Late Baroque abbey church. Engraving by Johann Haedener, about 1790.*

23

It is not widely known that in 1764–66 a circular chapel dedicated to the Guardian Angels (Schutzengelkapelle) was built north of the church nave. The unknown designer came from the region of Bregenz (Bregenzerwald).

Under Abbot Coelestin and his successor, Beda Angehrn (ruled 1767–1796), the *monastery square* was also extensively rebuilt. The Library, based on designs by PETER THUMB, was installed in the west wing in 1758/59. Brother GABRIEL LOSER was largely responsible for its spectacular decoration, while the ceiling paintings of 1762 carry the signature of JOSEF WANNENMACHER. In 1767 Abbot Beda undertook the construction of the long-planned *new palace* (Pfalz). The builder, FERDINAND BEER, succeeded in completing the construction of the present east wing of the administrative building in two years. Among the ceremonial rooms included in this building the throne room stood out in particular. It was painted in 1786/87 by ANTON PULLACHER, and became the present-day Great Council Chamber in 1880. The north wing, built on as an extension, remained uncompleted during the time of the monastery.

19th Century

Even though princely rule was abolished by the administration of the Canton of St.Gall in 1803, the development of the monastery square went on to its completion. At that time a number of medieval buildings such as the winehouse, the stables and the house of the brothers still stood along the northern flank, enclosed by the monastery wall. In 1808 the circular chapel of the Guardian Angels and probably at the same time the western part of the wall were demolished. In 1828, in place of the small gate opening towards the Kugelgasse, a vista was opened up which offered a new link between the Marktgasse and the monastery square. The inspiration for an integrated design for this

10 *North view of the monastery precinct before the construction of the north wing. Aquatint by Johann Baptist Isenring, 1836.*

northern area was the establishment of the joint diocese of Chur and St.Gall in 1824, that is, the prospect of an independent bishopric for St.Gall. An initial design was submitted by HANS CONRAD STADLER in 1831: a relatively short northern wing for the administrative building, a transversally placed chapel flanked by educational buildings, and a rectangular building for the canonical apartments, all in Classical style. In the same year, FELIX WILHELM KUBLY submitted a project which strove for greater enclosure of the monastery square. It is amazing that already at that time Kubly used the Tuscan pattern of the New Renaissance, which the architects LEO VON KLENZE and FRIEDRICH GAERTNER were utilising in Munich. When in 1833 the monastery chapter was abruptly terminated by the decision of the Great Council, another requirement came to the fore: a *cantonal arsenal.* This building, erected between 1838 and 1841, fitted in with the baroque wing of the square with regard to length and proportions. At the request of the Catholic administration, FELIX WILHELM KUBLY together with Stadler subsequently built the *Catholic School,* 1839–41 and, using his own designs, the *Children's Chapel* (Kinderkapelle), 1840/43.

The monastery square had now taken on its definitive form, which also successfully survived the new designs for the arsenal, of 1919/20 and 1962/63. Recently construction has largely taken place within this framework established in the 19th century.

The Monastery Square

The former abbey and the town are two unequal partners, which have stood facing each other like two poles for centuries, and have finally grown together into a grandiose unity while retaining their individual characters. Whereas the more distant Multergasse and Spisergasse, like the Schmiedgasse and Turmgasse, wrap themselves around the monastery like shells, in nearby Gallusstrasse one feels an architectural closedness, as if here the town had developed its own dynamics, not to say obstinacy. Gallusstrasse, into which side-roads lead, features broad areas with steps and only opened up to the square after the demolition of the partition walls, around 1808. Marktgasse also, which narrows funnel-like up to the church of Saint Laurence, has only led directly to the square since 1838. Here the visitor steps from the narrow medieval streets of the secular town into the baroque es-

11 The monastery square from the east with abbey church and palace wing; right, north wing and Kinderkapelle (Children's Chapel).

*12 Northern transverse gable of the rotunda with the arms of the abbot
and builder Coelestin Gugger, 1758.*

tablishment of a spiritual sovereign. *A three-wing complex,* dominated by the awesome *Cathedral,* encompasses the spacious, ordered square, with its simple lawns and geometric network of paths. The further one proceeds eastwards, the more powerfully the facade of the Cathedral rears up; its twin towers seem to spring from the ground, pointing towards Heaven, a grandiose embodiment of power and discipline, of architecture and sculpture. Facing it is the monumental new palace in Late Baroque style which has been the seat of the St.Gall cantonal administration since 1803. The southern flank consists of the prim old part of the abbey, the seat of the Bishop of St.Gall since 1847, and on the north side is the old 19th century arsenal, which since 1979 has housed the archives of the ecclesiastical foundation, the state archives, the cantonal administration library, the cantonal tribunal and other administrative departments. Finally, the Late Classical group of buildings, including the Children's Chapel and the school, acts as a connecting hinge with the town, which forms a picturesque backdrop to the west.

28

The Cathedral

Exterior

I. East facade, 1761–1764. The idea for the *twin-towered* ⑪ *facade,* which faces towards the residence and away from the town, was probably that of JOHANN CASPAR BAGNATO, 1750. However, the design in question (project XIII in the foundation archives) bears the handwriting of JOSEF ANTON FEUCHTMAYER, who was not only manually but also artistically talented. The wooden model, which differs slightly from this design, and which finally convinced both the abbot and the monastic community, is the work of Brother GABRIEL LOSER, 1752, and is found in the library. The construction was carried out under the direction of JOHANN MICHAEL BEER VON BILDSTEIN, the sculpturally «kneaded» sandstone facade suggesting the direct collaboration of JOSEF ANTON FEUCHTMAYER. The concave and convex forms of the two towers and the apse are especially noteworthy, as is the richly articulated orchestration of the columns and pilasters. On the balcony of the apse are sandstone statues of St.Desiderius and St.Mauritius, which are copies by ALFONS MAGG, made in about 1930; the originals, by JOHANN OECHSLIN, 1842, are now in the fountain courtyard (Brunnenhof). The stucco-like frontispiece relief in sandstone depicting the Assumption of the Blessed Virgin Mary is a free re-creation by Magg, 1934, of the Feuchtmayer original. The towers house a nine-part set of bells. In the north tower are two large bells made by PETER LUDWIG KAISER of Zug, 1767. In the south tower are bells by HIERONYMUS GESUS of Constance, 1616; JEAN GIRARD DE LA MOTTE of Lothringen, 1633; ANDREAS APORTA of Feldkirch, 1702 and 1707; JOHANN HEINRICH ERNST of Lindau, 1766; PETER LUDWIG KAISER, 1767; and LEONHARD ROSENLAECHER of

Constance, 1772. In the lanterns hang five more small bells by JOHANN BAPTIST APORTA of Bregenz, 1732; JOHANN LEONHARD ROSENLAECHER, 1783; JOHANN HEINRICH ERNST, 1766, and PETER ERNST, 1733; as well as an unsigned one, 1932. The clockwork, one of the largest in Switzerland, is in the north tower and actuates a total of eleven clocks in the church and precinct buildings; it was made by JOSEF ANTON LINDENMANN in 1763.

II. The nave and rotunda. The nave, covered by a gable roof, is relatively simple, with rounded arch windows. The rotunda, which projects in a semi-circle on each side, is covered by a mansard roof of which a wooden model is still kept in the Foundation building. The architectural motif of the rotunda, i.e. of a central unit transversally cutting through a longitudinal building, already occurs, for example, in a project by FRANZ BEER for Ottobeuren, probably before 1696. It is also shown in project XII in the Foundation archives, and is probably by PETER THUMB, 1749. The main portal, framed by co-

13 South side of the Cathedral with former monastery buildings and cloister-walk.

14 St.Gallus. Wood figure by Christian Wenzinger, 1758, Augsburg.
15 St.Benedict. Sandstone figure on the north rotunda.

lumns, opens in the centre of the north front. Above it is a bust of the Saviour (a copy by MAGG, the original by CHRISTIAN WENZINGER is now in the northern cloister-walk). *The door,* made in about 1810, is decorated in Classical style and has two reliefs: the giving of the keys to St.Peter and the expulsion from the Temple, modeled on an earlier design by the entourage of FRANZ ANTON DIRR. The lateral niches shelter figures: below, the two Princes of the Apostles, Peter and Paul, above, Gallus and Otmar. The gable bears the arms of the abbot and builder, Coelestin II Gugger von Staudach (1740–1767) ⑫ surmounted by the insignia of the abbot and surrounded by the chain of the Order of the Annunciation. On the opposite side, in similarly arranged niches, stand Sts. Benedict and Magnus, Eusebius and Notker. The gable bears a sandstone relief: St.Gallus and a bear with ro- ⑭

31

16 West gable of the Cathedral with statue of the Mother of God by Christian Wenzinger (copy by A. Magg).

caille, the work of CHRISTIAN WENZINGER. The wooden model for the figure of Gallus is in the municipal collection in Augsburg.

III. West facade. The strikingly plain west front has a large central projection which faces onto the Gallusplatz, originally encircled by the partition wall. The frontispiece, decorated with volutes, has a statue of the Blessed Virgin (a copy by MAGG); the original, by CHRISTIAN WENZINGER, is in the garden south of the nuns' wing.

⑮

The present vestibule to the entrance at the south-west corner was built in 1935; the wood reliefs are by JOSEF BUESSER, who also carved the northern double portal.

Interior

The design of the cathedral consists of a basilica with three naves and a central cupola. Massive pillars pierced by high arcades, so as to form the side aisles, support the tunnel vaults and the cupola of the rotunda. The spatial unity, the relationships of the various elements to each other, the light pouring in through the high windows, all combine to create an impression which is both solemn and serene. The Baroque concept of unifying a longitudinal church with a central construction is expressed here in an exemplary way. The sandstone and woodwork at the lower level of the church speak of the terrestial sphere. Above this the architecture develops in a radiant manner and holds in equilibrium the colourful altar decoration and the choir screen. In the intermediate zone, graceful stucco forms in malachite green dart out and up into the vaulting, where the ceiling paintings, with their wealth of figures, hang like wreaths of smoke. The clay-yellow stucco figures also send important colour accents into the green pendentives of the cupola and into the vaulting of the side aisles. The majesty of the architecture and the light-dark contrasts produce a solemn atmosphere, which is not spoiled by the Neo-classical west gallery and the somewhat pompous high altar, both added later.

1. West crypt. Below the gallery is the crypt of St.Otmar, which was built into the then already existing Otmar church by Abbot Ymmo (ruled 976–984). It survived the reconstruction of the Otmar church from 1623 to 1626 and also its demolition in 1758. The three-aisled, almost square crypt (approx. 6×6 m), which was originally approached from side galleries, is subdivided into

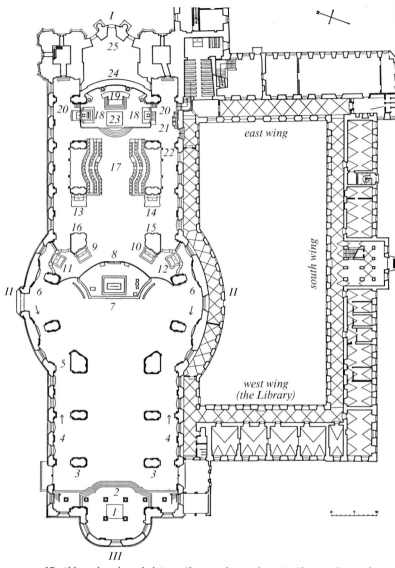

east wing

south wing

*west wing
(the Library)*

17 *Abbey church and cloister (former claustral area). The numbers refer to places in the text.*
18 *The abbey church to the east, with rotunda and monks' choir.* ▶

three naves by four columns and has a groined vault. The semicircular capitals with small lateral coils are unusual. The new altar block encloses the relics of Saint Otmar. On the walls of the choir are the *remains of Late Gothic frescoes,* from the second half of the 15th century: right, St.Elizabeth (?) and the martyrdom of St.Ursula at Cologne (?); left, St.Gallus with bread. The area in front is reserved as the burial place of the bishops of St.Gall (see p.214).

2. The gallery. The organ gallery, built by JOSEF SIMON MOOSBRUGGER as late as 1809/10, replaced three west altars. The stiff, Classical construction rests on six front columns and two back Tuscan columns and is reached by two spiral staircases. The organ plan conceived by Moosbrugger in 1811 originally included a monumental organ by FRANZ FROSCH and his son, of

19 *The abbey church towards the west, with chancel, 1786. The Classical organ platform was built in 1809/10 in place of the west choir.*

Munich. The present instrument behind an altered facade was made by the KUHN Company of Maennedorf in 1968.

3. Banner cabinets. Next to the pillars in the nave that is furthest to the rear stand two high cupboards with sculpted corners and painted imitation veneer, made about 1770–80. In the medallions are paintings of the busts of six apostles, with their attributes.

4. Confessionals. Along the walls of the side aisles and the rotunda stand eight confessionals on each side, made in 1761/63 by JOSEF ANTON FEUCHTMAYER with the collaboration of FRANZ ANTON DIRR. They consist of a three-part frame made of walnut, with richly sculpted and animated fronts, crowned by reliefs and busts, accompanied by putti. The themes are based on the sacrament of penance. The grisaille and gold reliefs were executed by JOSEF STAELZER in 1769. On the women's side, from the rear to the front: Jesus and the sinner, the wife of Canaan, Jesus and the Samaritan woman, the lost coin, Mary Magdalene, Eve, the Virgin [20] Mary, the penitent Margaretha von Cortona (1247–1297); on the men's side: Jesus and Zacchaeus, the tax collector and the Pharisee, the prodigal son, the Good Shepherd, Peter, Adam, the Sorrowing Christ and Paul. The carved sides of the renovated benches are by FIDEL SPORER, about 1760.

5. Pulpit. Marbled Rococo frame in Louis XVI style [21] by FRANZ ANTON DIRR, based on a design by JOSEF ANTON FEUCHTMAYER, 1786, executed by MATHIAS MADER. On the border of the pulpit sit the polished white figures of the four Evangelists with their attributes (Luke, John, Matthew, Mark), showing the opening texts of their respective Gospels. Between them is a relief of St.Notker in combat with the Devil in the form of a dog,

20 Confessional on the women's side, relief of the penitent Mary Magdalene, 1761–63, by Josef Anton Feuchtmayer and Franz Anton Dirr. ▶

37

22 St.Gallus makes known the word of God. Clay model by Christian Wenzinger, 1758, in the Augustine Museum Freiburg im Breisgau.

St.Gallus and St.Otmar against a background of the landscape of Lake Constance with the town of Bregenz and two skiffs, and the beheading of St.Eusebius. Above the pulpit door, the inscription: QUI EX DEO EST VERBA DEI AUDIT, John VIII, 47 (He who is of God, hears the words of God). On the sounding board, putti with sheep and a dog, surmounted by the Good Shepherd with a halo.

6. Gallus series, in stucco. In the side spaces of the rotunda are yellow wall reliefs with Latin titles, which are from the hand of CHRISTIAN WENZINGER, 1755/57. On the south side (from front to rear): MERCES OPE-RARII (The labourer's wage). Gallus receives the letter of protection for the monastery from the Frankish king, Sigisbert. SACRIFICIUM IUSTITIAE (The sacrifice of

◄ *21 Chancel by Franz Anton Dirr, 1786, after a sketch by Josef Anton Feuchtmayer. Transition style to Louis XVI.*

justice). Gallus celebrates the holy sacrifice of the Mass. VERBUM SALUTIS (The Holy Word). Gallus spreads the Word of God. There is a clay model of this relief in the Augustine Museum in Freiburg-im-Breisgau. VIS- CERA MISERICORDIAE (Heart filled with compassion). Gallus gives alms. On the north side: VESTIMEN-

23 Stucco relief based on the model, in the south rotunda, about 1758, by Christian Wenzinger.

24 Mary altar in the rotunda, 1769–72, painting by Stefano Maria Legnani from Milan, 1691.
25 Epitaph for the Prince-Abbot and Cardinal Coelestin Sfondrati (d. 1696), put up about 1780.

TUM SALUTIS (The holy robe). Gallus hands over the veil of the Order to the duchess Fridiburga. ZELUS DOMINI (Wrath of the Lord). Destruction of the idols upon Gallus' arrival in Tuggen. BENEDICTIO PATRIS (The Father's blessing). The departing Columban blesses Gallus, who remains behind. MORI LUCRUM (Death is victory). Death of St.Gallus. For the stucco allegories below the cupola see p.75.

7. Officiating altar. New construction of 1967 designed by HANS BURKARD, St.Gall.

⑱   *8. Choir screen.* Made in 1772 by the palace ironsmith JOSEF MAYER of Buetschwil after a design by FRANZ ANTON DIRR. The screen, which stretches like a curtain from pillar to pillar in nine sections, is made of green rods into which gold tendrils and flowers are woven like lace, filling and overflowing the upper border. In

26 *Gathering of manna. Cast bronze relief by Franz Anton Dirr, about 1770, on the altar of the Herz-Jesu-Chapel (Sacred Heart Chapel).*

the centre is a surmounting round arch crowned with the arms of the Prince-Abbot Beda Angehrn (ruled 1767–1796), encircled by the chain of the Order of the Annunciation and accompanied by the pontifical insignia.

9–12. Side altars in the rotunda. Stucco and marble retables, rather small in relation to the surrounding area, in reddish-white alabaster, by FIDEL SPORER, 1769–72. The four altars face each other as matching pieces. The outside two have side columns and connecting bridges to the pillars, the inside ones have only curved pilasters but with a somewhat more luxuriant top. The bases have cast bronze plaques with figures by FRANZ ANTON DIRR. The Old Testament sacrificial scenes allude to the sacrifice of the mass. A fifth relief is in the Herz Jesu Kapelle (Sacred Heart Chapel) (p.134). The altar patron saints were changed after the removal of the west choir altars in 1809. *9. Holy Cross altar.* Crucifixion paintings by XAVER HECHT, 1809, in the upper part, Saint Peter. Neo-

Baroque tabernacle, end of 19th century. On the base is a plaque showing the meeting between Abraham and Melchizedek. *10. Altar of the Virgin Mary.* Excellent painting of the Blessed Virgin, 1691, by STEFANO MARIA LEGNANI, Milan. (Abbot Coelestin I Sfondrati, the abbot at that time, was from Milan.) Upper part, Saint Paul. On the base a relief showing Abraham's sacrifice. *11. Otmar altar.* Painting, perhaps by JOSEF KELLER of Pfronten, about 1815, above, Saint Valentine. On the base, a relief showing the sacrifices of Cain and Abel. On the curved bridging sections at the sides, polished white statues of St.Maurice (putto with a sword) and St.Sebastian with an arrow. On the nearby choir pillar hangs a Late Baroque painting of Gallus, which must formerly have adorned the Gallus altar. *12. Gallus altar.* Painting by JOSEF KELLER, 1810. Above, St.Magnus, by SEVERIN BENZ, mid-19th century. On the base, a relief showing Noah's offering. On the bridges, Ulrich (putto with a fish) and Konrad (attribute missing). Next to the altar, the *small Gallus bell* made of steel sheeting can be rung with a clapper. Its old-fashioned shape resembles that of a goat bell. It bears an 18th-century painting of Gallus, with the German inscription: «Saint Gallus used this bell in his residence, known as Gallenstein, near Bregenz, in the year 612.». This small bell, donated by Bregenz to St.Gall in 1786, may quite possibly date back to the early Middle Ages. On the nearby pillar is a Late Baroque painting of St.Benedict from an altar that no longer exists.

13. and 14. Choir altars. The two artificial marble retables by JOSEF ANTON FEUCHTMAYER, 1763, which were conceived as a matching pair, originally stood to the sides of the choir stalls or the thrones and were moved to the pillars in about 1808. *13. Altar of St.John.* The painting by ORAZIO MORETTO, about 1810–20, shows John the Evangelist with the Angel of the Apocalypse. *14. Altar of St.Notker.* The painting shows St.Notker in his legendary combat with the Devil, which took place in the nearby crypt of St.Columban. Painted about 1770 by MARTIN KNOLLER after a sketch in the Baroque Museum of Salzburg, this very good picture originally hung over the present Gallus altar (no. 12 above).

15. Epitaph for Prince-Abbot Coelestin I Sfondrati ㉕ *(ruled 1687–1696) from Milan.* On 12 December 1695 the learned abbot was appointed a cardinal, whereupon he resigned his position at St.Gall. However, shortly afterwards, on 4 September 1696, he died in Rome and was laid to rest in his titular church, Santa Cecilia. Father Hermann Schenk brought his heart back to St.Gall, where it was buried in the abbey church. The Classical epitaph depicts the personal arms of the prelate, accompanied by symbols of transience, a skull, a broken candle, an hourglass and a torch. Above the inscription tablet, the pontifical insignia and cardinal's hat. The tablet reads: Hic Requiescit / COR / COELESTINI SFONDRATI / S.R.I. Princip. Abbat. S.Galli / S.R.E. Cardinalis Presbyt. Tit. / S. Caeciliae.Cui / Avorum Gloria. Propria Virtute / Libris editis Clarissimo de DEO / Ecclesia. Monasterio Scriptis / & Gestis optime Merito. Sed / Praematuris Fatis Ao MDCXCVI. Die IV. Septembr. Aetatis LIII. / Expectationi Urbis & Orbis erepto / Hoc gratae memoriae Monumentum / in hac nova Basilica / BEDA princeps / posuit. (Here rests the heart of Prince-Abbot Coelestin Sfondrati, cardinal priest of Santa Cecilia, who was greatly renowned for his personal virtues and his publications, for God, the Church and the monastery, and for his most worthy writings and deeds, but was prematurely torn away from the expectations of Rome and the world on 4 September 1696, at the age of 53. This memorial is erected in grateful remembrance of him in this new church by Prince-Abbot Beda [Angehrn].)

16. Epitaph for Prince-Abbot Coelestin Gugger von Staudach (ruled 1740–1767), builder of this church. The

27 *Choir stalls; dorsal reliefs: left, Benedict receives the habit of the order from the hand of Romanus (north 2). Right, Benedict unmasks Riggo, who claims to be the King of the Goths (south 10).*

layout is the same as for no. 15. The inscription reads: COELESTINO II. / S.R.I. Principi Abbati S.Galli & S.Joannis / in Valle Thurae Comiti Doggenburgi. / Regii Ord. Annunt. Virg. Equiti. / Postquam / Iura Monasterii simulque Pacem mira / Prudentia per Annos XXVI. servasset. / Territorium V. Paroeciis. Clerum novis / Beneficiis. Monasterium Aedificiis auxisset. / Orbi litterato Bibliothecam, Publico / Bono Domum Frumentariam. Su / perum Cultui hanc Basilicam / erexisset: / Compositis subditorum Dissidiis. / Firmata cum Epu Constantiensi Concordia. / Pacis studiis immortuo / Anno MDCCLXVII. Die XXIV. Februarii. / Aetatis LXVI. / Hoc gratitudinis Monumentum / Meritissimo Moerens Successor / Posuit. / Patrem Optimum / Lugete Posteri. (To the imperial Prince and Abbot Coelestin II. of St.Gall and St.Johann in the Toggenburg Thurtal, knight of the Order of the Annunciation. After protecting the rights of the monastery and also peace with amazing wisdom for 26 years, enriching his land with five new parishes, the clergy with new foundations and the monastery with new constructions, providing the academic world with the Library, the public welfare with a granary [in Rorschach], after establishing this church for the worship of the Almighty, after overcoming all obstacles with his subordinates and after signing the Concordat with the bishop of Constance, he died in the midst of his untiring efforts for peace, on 24 February 1767, at the age of 66. This memorial to the most worthy abbot is placed here by his successor. The best of fathers, mourned by his children.)

17. *Choir stalls and organs.* The walnut choir stalls, aranged in two sections of three rows each, making a total of 84 seats, are a major work by JOSEF ANTON FEUCHTMAYER, who was responsible in particular for the basic form and the dorsal reliefs. He was assisted by

28 Choir stalls on south side by Feuchtmayer, Dirr and Loser; choir organs by Viktor Ferdinand and Josef Bossard, 1768–70.

the wood-carvers JOHANN GEORG and FRANZ ANTON DIRR, the cabinet maker Brother GABRIEL LOSER (intarsia) and the painter JOSEF STAELZER (execution of the reliefs). Above the dorsal wall of the stalls on either side two free-standing, symmetrical organ cases face each other; the pipes rise upwards and out to the encompassing pilasters of the choir, the centre remaining free. The creators of these unusual organs were VIKTOR FERDINAND and JOSEF BOSSARD of Baar (Zug), 1768–70. The crowning putti and musical angels are by FRANZ ANTON DIRR. The central statues of Gallus and Otmar date from the late 17th century and, according to the most recent findings, come from the former gate of the palace wing. The dorsal reliefs of the stalls depict *scenes from the life*
⑳ *of St.Benedict.* Their sequence from east to west jumps irregularly from one side to the other, according to the following numbering: *North side:* 2. Romanus gives the habit of the Order to the young Benedict. 3. Temptation by a girl in Subiaco. 6. Benedict orders the monk Maurus to pull the drowning Placidus from the water. 7. Benedict destroys the idols on Montecassino. 9. Benedict receives the messenger who brings him the sad news of the
㉘ death of Bishop Germanus from Capua. *South side:* 1. The young Benedict kneels before the miraculous image of Piscinola. 4. An attempt to poison Benedict in Vicovaro does not succeed. 5. The senators Tertullus and Equitius give their sons Placidus and Maurus to Benedict. 8. Benedict drives away the Evil One. 10. Benedict unmasks the warlord Riggo, who claims to be King Totila of the Goths.

18. Thrones. The two mighty thrones which stand before the high altar belonged to the abbot (now to the bishop) and to the dean (now to the officiating priest). They were originally placed diagonally to the west of the choir stalls and were hidden by the Feuchtmayer altars (see nos. 13 and 14). Reliefs: left, death of St.Benedict; right, death of St.Scholastica, the sister of Benedict. Be-

29 *High altar by Josef Simon Moosbrugger, 1808–10, paintings about 1644/45; in the apse cupola, paintings by Josef Keller, 1809/10.*

hind the left throne, Neo-Renaissance altar with paintings of St.Eusebius, end of 19th century. On the opposite side, a Baroque painting of Pentecost, mid-18th century.

19. High altar. The powerful retable of black and grey artificial marble, which fills the east apse, was the work of JOSEF SIMON MOOSBRUGGER, 1808–10. The large altar design of about 1760 by Brother GABRIEL LOSER, now in the Library, remained unexecuted. The angel figures are by JOSEF SPORER of Constance, the crown by JOHANN NEPOMUK STIPPELDEY of Augsburg. The monumental painting of the Ascension of the Blessed Virgin Mary (6.2×3.5 m) is a masterpiece by ㉙ GIOVANNI FRANCESCO ROMANELLI of Viterbo, about 1644/45, and was a gift from Cardinal Giovanni Francesco Barberini to Abbot Pius Reher. The upper right hand corner was completed in 1810 by JOSEF KELLER, who also painted the apse.

20. Stucco reliefs. On the eastern front walls of the side aisles are two reliefs with figures which differ in style from the Wenzinger stucco groups in the rotunda. The one on the north shows St.Otmar standing in front of two singing monks at a lectern which bears the inscrip- ㉛ tion: SIC STEMUS (Thus we stand). At the top of the blind arch, rocaille with the inscription: LAETOS FECIT CANTORES (Let the singers be joyful). On the south side we see the artist-monk Tuotilo with his palette and paintbrushes, with Notker and another brother.

21. Celebrant's prayer stool. This unusual piece with its four prayer niches is decoratively carved on the convex ends, and has reliefs of figures on the kneeling-benches: the Mount of Olives the carrying of the Cross, Crucifixion and the Lamentation. Workshop of DIRR about 1770.

22. Remains of the Gothic choir. During the restoration of the church, parts of the south wall of the Gothic choir were retained. In the course of the restoration traces of painted crosses (1483) were found, one of which was left on view. Next to the present exit to the cloister, a piece of the arch of the original Gothic portal has been

30 *Lamentation of Christ in the presence of St.Otmar. Remains of a wall painting in a niche on the exterior of the choir, 1521 (?).* ▶

31 St.Otmar and two singing monks. Stucco relief in the north side aisle of the choir, about 1770.

exposed. On the outer wall to the right of the portal (i.e. in the cloister-walk), a *Late Gothic fresco* can be seen in a lunette cut in half: the lamentation of Christ in Zeeland; right, St.Otmar with a small cask, book, crosier and mitre. At the top of the arch, the arms of Roesch, dated 1521 (?). Very probably the fresco belongs to the tomb of Abbot Ulrich Roesch (ruled 1463–1491), which was destroyed during the Reformation. However, the late date remains problematical.

23. East crypt. The east crypt is dedicated to St.Columban and its foundations date from the 9th century. It underwent a transformation at the time of the construction of the church. In 1767 four new Tuscan columns were placed in the square hall and an unsegmented barrel vault with lunettes was erected. Since the most recent restorations, the niche in the north-east corner has contained the remains of the three last abbots: Coelestin Gugger von Staudach (ruled 1740–1767), Beda Angehrn (ruled 1767–1796) and Pankratius Vorster (ruled 1796–1805, d. 1829).

24. Lower sacristy. The space behind the end of the choir, between the two towers, arches outwards to the east, so that, from the outside, one has the impression that this is the apse of the choir. The shallow-domed vault with lunettes is decorated along its borders by heavily overpainted stucco rocaille from the GIGL workshop and has a new ceiling painting, signed «O. Haemmerle, Munich Solln 1931». This painting shows the sacrifice of Abraham and Melchizedeck and emblems of the mass. In the sacristy there are excellent wall cupboards made of walnut, their fronts decorated with reliefs of vines, from the monastery workshop, about 1770. In the window niche, above a pewter washstand, is an Early Baroque crucifixion group of the first half of the 17th century; the ironwork dates from the 18th century.

25. Upper sacristy. A staircase originally used by the monks leads from the south-east corner of the choir to the first floor of the east section of the monastery, where a gallery provides access to the upper sacristy. Here too we find a shallow-arch vault with large-scale Rococo stucco decorations from the GIGL workshop. The fir and oak wood flooring is laid in the shape of two large stars, reminiscent of the floor in the Library. The *Renaissance* ㉜ *wall cupboards* and parament chests, which came from the old church building, are surprising. Despite their uniform appearance, they have obviously been reassembled and in some cases cut here and there. The veneer fronts, crowned with friezes and separated by moulding, are decorated with various arches: some, which look like triumphal arches, consist of rather flat appliqués with volutes and strapwork motifs, and perhaps still belong to the 16th century; others have strongly three dimensional supports and volute crowns, and date from 1613. This date is to be found on a lock in the middle of the front part of the western cupboard, accompanied by the initials I M. The locksmith is unknown, but the cabinet maker was probably HANS JOERG DOERIG of Wil, who was at that time overseer of all the construction work of the monastery, including that at Rorschach and St.Johann. In 1623/24 he was also involved in the decoration of the Otmar church (including the confessionals) and in 1628 he made the panelling in the abbot's room in the monastery of Neu St.Johann. The possibility that the

32 Upper sacristy. Renaissance wall cupboard with rich decoration, dated 1613, probably from the Wil workshop.

54

sacristy cupboards originated in Wil is also suggested by a magnificent very similar cupboard from the former guildhall in Wil, now in the courthouse there.

The Church Treasure (no access)

Earlier inventories show that even before the end of the first millennium, the monastery of St.Gall already possessed a considerable church treasure, comparable with the collection still preserved today in Saint Maurice (Valais). Apart from precious relics, there were 76 mass vestments and 32 copes! In subsequent centuries additions were made to the church treasure. Items were sometimes sold. At the time of the *destruction of the images at St.Gall,* in 1529, almost all the objects made of precious metal made their way to the mint or into commerce, so that the loss to the monastery was estimated to be about 30,000 gulden. During the Baroque period the sacristy was replenished. Thanks to the illustrated records «Sacrarium Sancti Galli» of Father Gregor Schnyder, 1699, and «De sacra suppellectili et alia» of Father Ambros Epp, 1785 (Library Mss. 1719 and 1722), we have an excellent idea today of the extent of the church treasure and of the reliquaries shortly before the dissolution of the monastery. Much was lost at the time of the founding of the Helvetic Republic and after the establishment of the Canton.

From the *pre-Reformation period* only *random individual pieces* remain, including a bowl with an engraved relief of Gallus, two reliquary horns, one processional cross, all about 1500, one pax tablet, dated 1510, and a small Otmar reliquary in the form of a box, probably from the 15th century. An ivory horn with the inscription «Nortbertus», probably Abbot Nortbert (ruled 1034–1072), stored in the Swiss National Museum in Zurich, was stolen.

Of the 17th century *silver figures,* of which formerly there were 15, only the statues of the Foundation patrons

Gallus and Otmar, made in 1623 by JOHANN JAKOB BAUR in Augsburg, still exist, as well as two later Rococo figures of the Princes of the Apostles, Peter and Paul, made in 1747–49 by FRANZ THADDAEUS LANG in Augsburg. Of the 27 chalices illustrated in 1785, 14 can be found in the inventory. Today, there are again more than *30 chalices* made before 1850, including pieces which were bought, such as a Late Gothic *tower-shaped ciborium* from Kappel (St.Gall). Among the donors were some abbots, such as Otmar Kunz, who gave a chalice of 1577 (probably made by JOHANNES RENNER in Wil); Coelestin Sfondrati, 1687; Josef von Rudolphi 1720/22, made by FRANZ IGNAZ BERTOLD in Augsburg; Pankraz Vorster, 1777, marked by JOSEF ANTON SEETHALER in Augsburg. Members of the monastery also donated chalices: Father Beatus Seiler, in about 1685, made by JOHANN LUDWIG WIELAND in Wil; Father Augustin Zagot of Freiburg (Switzerland), 1689 (by the same goldsmith of Wil); Father Chrysostomous Hailand of Fuessen, about 1730, by JOHANN GEORG HERKOMER; Father Honorat Peyer im Hof of Lucerne, 1735, by BEAT J. SCHUMACHER in Lucerne; Father Innozenz Herter von Hertler of Constance, 1738, by FRANZ THADDAEUS LANG in Augsburg; Father Athanasius von Benz of Radolfzell, 1750, by FRANZ IGNAZ BERTOLD in Augsburg; Father Karl Haug of Ueberlingen, 1750, by JOHANN WILHELM GUTWEIN in Augsburg, and Father Blasius Immenot of Feldkirch, 1774, by FRANZ ANTON BUESEL in St.Fiden near St.Gall.

Of the three ostensories, the «rich» monstrance in magnificent Louis XVI style, made in 1781/83 by JOSEF ANTON SEETHALER in Augsburg, is especially noteworthy; inset topaz with an engraving of the Crucifixion, and an enamel pelican, 16th century. The «ordinary» monstrance is also from the workshops of SEETHALER. The purchased third monstrance, from the Baroque period, is the work of JOHANN JOACHIM LUTZ (d.1727) in Augs-

33 Liturgical vestment made of parchment, prepared in 1685 for Abbot Gallus Alt, painted and decorated with writing by Father Gabriel Hecht.

burg. Among the numerous *crucifixes* the Renaissance processional cross of 1582, made by JOHANNES RENNER in Wil, stands out. There are also two small silver *reliquary altars* from Milan and from the Appenzell Workshop of FIDEL RAMSPERG, 1662, respectively, and, lastly, a 17th century *crosier* with antique cameos.

The approximately *30 Baroque vestments,* including seven vestments in several parts (chasubles, pluvials, dalmatics), and the corresponding chalice veils are particularly precious. A *parchment vestment* of 1685 is unique, covered in writing and richly painted by Father GABRIEL HECHT. The theological and emblematic micro-writing which covers the entire surface has remained largely unsesearched until now.

③

The ceiling paintings

All of the paintings, except for those at the top of the dome, are the work of JOSEF WANNENMACHER of Tomerdingen (Wuertt.). He worked in the nave and in the rotunda, partly according to designs by Christian Wenzinger, 1757–1760, and in the choir, 1764–1766. The apse was painted by JOSEF KELLER of Pfronten in the Allgaeu only when the high altar was built in 1809/10. The additions painted by ANTONI DICK during the first restoration of the cupola in 1773 can no longer be distinguished. At the time of the restoration of 1966/67 the new paintings in the choir, by ORAZIO MORETTO, 1817–1823, and the overpainting by the BERTLE Brothers in the nave, 1866/67, were entirely removed. The Wannenmacher frescoes were revealed in amazingly good condition, but required retouching here and there.

JOSEF WANNENMACHER brings on a host of saints. With the exception of a few architectural set pieces, he

34 *Plan of the ceiling pictures in the abbey church. The numbers refer to the text.* ▶

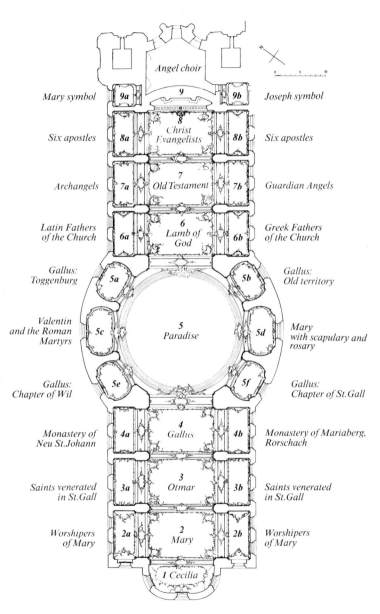

Angel choir

Mary symbol — 9a — 9 — 9b — Joseph symbol

8
Christ
Six apostles — 8a — Evangelists — 8b — Six apostles

7
Archangels — 7a — Old Testament — 7b — Guardian Angels

6
Latin Fathers — 6a — Lamb of — 6b — Greek Fathers
of the Church — God — of the Church

Gallus: — 5a — 5b — Gallus:
Toggenburg — Old territory

5
Valentin — Mary
and the Roman — 5c — Paradise — 5d — with scapulary and
Martyrs — rosary

Gallus: — 5e — 5f — Gallus:
Chapter of Wil — Chapter of St.Gall

4
Monastery of — 4a — Gallus — 4b — Monastery of Mariaberg,
Neu St.Johann — Rorschach

3
Saints venerated — 3a — Otmar — 3b — Saints venerated
in St.Gall — in St.Gall

2
Worshipers — 2a — Mary — 2b — Worshipers
of Mary — of Mary

1 Cecilia

59

avoids the illusionist painting so beloved at that time. Profound religious conviction lies at the heart of this work. The further one penetrates into the world of these images, the more clearly one senses their iconographical importance. They testify to Benedictine erudition, but are ultimately subordinate to a theological explanation. The records of Brother Mathias Jansen (1738–1781) provide welcome assistance in identifying most of the saints, even though here and there a question mark remains.

For better identification, the description of the paintings includes the stucco groups of frolicking allegorical figures in the vault, which, in the rotunda in particular, are interrelated with them iconographically.

The nave
1. Former west choir. Inscription on the arch of the vault: MEMOR ESTO CONGREGATIONIS TUAE (Remember thy congregation, Psalm 74,2). In the vault bay cut by lateral lunettes we see, above the organ, the monogram of the Virgin in Glory. Below this we see St.Cecilia playing the organ, accompanied by two singers in Benedictine habit and angels with musical instruments.

㉟ 2. TEMPLUM INNOCENTIAE VIRGINI IMMACULATAE DIVOQUE OTHMARO DICATUM (The house of God is consecrated to the sinless and immaculate Virgin and to Saint Otmar). In the centre, the Virgin Mary, enthroned on a cloud, crushes the head of the serpent. She is surrounded by angels carrying the emblems of purity and virginity: a garland of flowers, the fleece of Gideon (Judges 6,37), a sceptre with the inscription «non pro te» (not for you), the answer to the serpent «sed pro omnibus» (but for all), Aaron's flowering rod (Numbers 17,8), a mirror and a lily. The arms below and to the left belong to the Abbot and Cardinal Coelestin Sfondrati

35 Veneration of the Immaculate Virgin Mary. ▶
36 Otmar and the St.Gall domains Ebringen and Neuravensburg. ▶

EARUM PRINCIPEM
VIRGINI IMMACULATAE
ROMAE OTTIMBAO
PRAEBAT

MEMOR ESTO
CONGREGATIONIS
TUAE

POST
MVNDILIO EUROPA
VENERVNTO ROMA
VULPRIO IPOCRITI

APOSTOLUS
ALLEMANNAE

(ruled 1687–1696). The open book with the title «Innocentia Vindicata» is a reference to Sfondrati's work on the Immaculate Conception (St.Gall, 1695). Below right, arms of the builder, Abbot Coelestin Gugger von Staudach (ruled 1740–1767). Between two angels with the motto of the Virgin Mary «PRO TE – A TE» is a throne with the chain of the Savoyard Order of the Annunciation, which Abbot Gallus Alt was the first to receive, in 1686.

2a. HONORIFICATA (The chosen one [wisdom gives eternal fame, Jesus Sirach 15,2]). Three special venerators and supporters of the Immaculate Conception are depicted here: in the middle, with the book «SINE MACULA», the Benedictine Doctor of the Church, Anselm of Canterbury (1033/34–1109), whose tract «De conceptione sanctae Mariae» considerably promoted devotion to the Immaculate Conception, although the dogma was only proclaimed in 1854; left, Archbishop Ildefons of Toledo (d. 667) with a lily rod and Hebraic inscription, probably referring to his work «De virginitate S. Mariae contra tres infideles»; right, the Venerable Bede (672/73–735), the Doctor of the Church who disseminated the Psalterium Marianum in England. The Greek scroll *ΘΕΟΤΟΚΟΣ* (Mother of God) refers to the definition of Mary at the Council of Ephesus in 431. Anselm and Bede are also to be found in the Library (pp.106, 109). Above the window capital, putti with sceptre, a garland of roses and a crown, attributes of Mary, Queen of Heaven.

^{⑥¹}

^{⑷²}

2b. BENEDICTA (Blessed). The central figure is Pope Gregory the Great (reigned 590–604), with the dove of the Holy Ghost sitting on his shoulder. (The head of Gregory is a portrait of the Bishop of St.Gall Joseph Hasler, 1964). An angel holds the text of the Easter hymn «REGINA COELI LAETARE ALLELUJA», which is said to have resounded during a rogation. The accompanying musical notes remind one of this pope's contribution to church music (Gregorian chant). Left, below, sits Cardinal Petrus Damiani (1006/7–1072), of the Benedictine order. He promoted monastic devotion to the Virgin Mary with his «OFFICIUM MINUS B(EATAE) V(IR-GINIS)». On the right, the Reichenau monk Hermann the Lame (Hermanus Contractus) (1013–1054), who was renowned as a great scholar and is thought to have written the «SALVE REGINA REDEMPTORIS MATER». Above the capital, putti- drummer and trumpeter.

3. The inscription «APOSTOLUS ALEMANNIAE» in the fourth vault bay appears to refer to St.Gallus. Here we see St.Otmar floating with open arms on a cloud, surrounded by angels bearing a pectoral cross, mitre and crosier, the insignia of the founder of the abbey, as well

37 The Mother of God and Gallus as protectors of the Monastery.

38 St.Eusebius and other saints. Oil sketch by Christian Wenzinger (?) in the Monastery of St.Paul in Lavanttal (Carinthia).

as a cask, paten and a glass filled with water. An angel holds up a scroll: «HIC EST FRATRUM AMATOR ET POPULI II. Mac.» (He is the friend of the brothers and of the people, 2. Mac. 15,14). Below him an angel opens a book: «AUSCULTA O FILI ECCE LEX Reg.S.B.» (Hear, my son, this is the rule of Saint Benedict). Next to this are two maps with, in the corners, the arms of the St.Gall possessions of Ebringen and Neuravensburg, which, as isolated domains in the territory north of the Rhine and Lake Constance, required the special protection of the heavenly powers.

⊛   3a. FIRMAMENTUM VIRTUTIS ([The Lord is] a powerful protector, Jesus Sirach 34,19). Here the minor patrons of the monastery of St.Gall are depicted. In the centre, Eusebius (d. 884) with open arms, accompanied by a small angel with a scythe; in 882 he succeeded in arranging for his monastery cell on the Viktorsberg in Vorarlberg to be incorporated into the monastery of St.Gall. Left, St.Ulrich (d. 973), Bishop of Augsburg. The fish on the book recall the legend of meat turning into fish on a Friday. Right, St.Remaclus in bishop's robes. This contemporary of St.Gallus was a monk and abbot in Luxeuil (Stablo in the Netherlands), where he died in about 670/76. Before him, a fountain from which issues a snake. The veneration of Remaclus must have been in-

39 St.Eusebius and other saints. Completed ceiling painting in the second bay of the north side aisle.

troduced at St.Gall during the time of Abbot Nortbert (ruled 1034–1072), who originally came from Stablo. Behind him, the St.Gall recluse Wiborada, who was killed by the Hungarians in 926. The design for this ceiling painting is preserved in the monastery of St.Paul in the Lavanttal (Carinthia, Austria). Above the capital, two putti with a pile of books.

3b. PROTECTIO FORTIS ([A true friend] is a strong fortress, Jesus Sirach 6,14). The painting depicts Notker the Stammerer (ca. 840–912), a monk of St.Gall, who was beatified in 1513. The broken rod refers to the legendary combat of the saint with the Devil in the form of a dog. Left, St.Magnus (699–772), first a monk at St.Gall, then founder of the monastery of Fuessen in the Allgaeu. His staff was carried over the fields as protection against insect plagues. The bishop in front of him is Constantius, who was martyred in about 165 and whose relics were brought from Rome to Constance by Abbot-Bishop Salomon in 904. On the right, St.Fides, the legendary martyr venerated in Conques (Dep. of Aveyron in France), and also from 1085 at St.Gall. The gridiron recalls her martyrdom. The design for this ceiling picture is also in the monastery of St.Paul in the Lavanttal (Carinthia, Austria). Above the capital, two putti embody the triumph of the Cross over the dragon.

65

4. APOSTOLUS ALEMANNIAE. The «Alemannic apostle» is apparently St.Gallus, not – as assumed until now – St.Otmar. With outspread arms, St.Gallus, recognizable by the bear, reliquary bag and staff, commends the monastery to the Virgin. The appearance of the abbey church is as it was in 1760: it still has the Gothic choir. The inscription reads: «HAEC REQUIES IN SAECULUM SAECI» (This is my resting place for ever; here will I dwell. Psalm 132,14). In the centre of the circle of angels: left, the Princes of the Apostles, Peter and Paul, right, the martyrs Maurice and Bishop Desiderius of Cahors (ca. 590–655?), who can also be seen on the east façade as minor patrons of the monastery.

4a. SALUS DOMUI HUIC (Today salvation has come to this house, Luke 19,9). In the centre we see the Lamb of God, with an angel collecting the blood which drips from the wound in his side. The Lamb of God is the heraldic symbol of the monastery of St.Johann in the Thurtal, which was incorporated into the monastery of St.Gall in 1555 and was rebuilt in the Sidwald as Neu St.Johann in about 1629/30. An angel presents a picture of this new monastery. To the right, the evangelist St.John, with an eagle, and John the Baptist with outstretched hand, as though saying: «Ecce Agnus Dei» (Behold the Lamb of God). To the far left, the saint of the catacomb, St.Theodore, whose bones were solemnly transferred to the new monastery church of St.Johann in 1685. Above the capital, two putti with a crosier.

4b. FIRMAT DOMOS FILIORUM (He builds the houses of the sons, Sir. 3,11). St.Benedict, with cross and poison cup, blesses the monastery of Mariaberg in Rorschach, which, planned as a replacement for the monastery of St.Gall was built under Abbot Ulrich Roesch starting in 1487, but was subsequently used only for administrative purposes. An angel displays the plan of the monastery. Left, St.Columban (d. 615) with the attribute of the sun on his breast; below him the Roman martyr

Constantius, whose bones were transferred to the nunnery of Rorschach in 1674. Above the window capital, putti with the pontifical insignia and a sword, symbols of the spiritual and worldly power of the Prince-Abbot.

5. The cupola (40)
The two inscriptions in the transverse arches of the cupola towards the nave and towards the choir appear to relate to the paintings in the cupola. On the west side: «IN CHRISTO JESU PER EVANGELIUM EGO VOS GENUI» (I have begotten you in Jesus Christ through the Gospel, I. Cor. 4,15). On the east side: «CONTINET HOC SANCTUM SANCTORUM MILLIA TEMPLUM» (This holy house encloses a thousand saints). Saints in Paradise are depicted in the cupola. In the centre we see the *Holy Trinity* with the dove of the Holy Ghost at the top, God the Father and God the Son, to whom a nearby angel carries the mighty Cross of Salvation. *The Virgin Mary and John the Baptist* appear as intercessors for men (the «deesis»). In the same circle of clouds and angels we see *St. Joseph,* the spouse of Mary, with a lily, and at the foot of the cross, *Joachim and Anna,* the parents of Mary, identified by two small doves which refer to the gift presented to the Temple on her birth. The three figures embody the transition from the Old to the New Testament.

The saints themselves are divided into eight groups, corresponding to the eight beatitudes of the Sermon on the Mount, the Latin texts of which are to be seen within the cartouches at the border of the cupola. Identification is based partly on dress and attributes, and partly on the record of Brother Mathias Jansen (1738–1781). After the restoration which took place in the 1960s all 60 saints are now once again visible; some of them had previously been covered up. Even though they appear to have been arranged in an orderly manner in three circles of cloud, the individual groups have a pyramidal formation, very

42 Saints venerating the Immaculate Conception of Mary. First bay in the south side aisle.

dense in the eastern half and sparser in the western half. Saints from the Benedictine order predominate, appearing particularly often in the upper circle, but we also see the founders of other orders, as well as individual women and even representatives of the Old Testament. Most are saints who were linked to the monastery of St.Gall, but there also appear very rare saints, who perhaps provide the key to the iconographic source. It has still to be determined who was responsible for the conception of the somewhat unusual sequence of saints.

BEATI PAUPERES SPIRITU (Blessed are the poor in spirit). Above the triumphal arch, which, together with a balustrade, stands out as the only architectural motif, we see *Gallus*[1] and *Columban*[2], the first with a white beard and a bear, the second with the traditional sun attribute on his breast. The group of figures on the left begins with the kneeling *Francis*[3], recognizable by his stigmata. The large figure of a prelate above him is that of *Coelestin V*[4], who, as an 80-year old monk ascended the throne of St.Peter for five months in 1294 and was deposed by Boniface VIII. He died in prison and was canonized in 1313. Coelestin appears here as a substitute for the builder, Prince-Abbot Coelestin Gugger von Staudach (1740–1767). The kneeling hermit with a rosary and raised right hand is *Nicholas of Flue*[5], whose cult in Swit-

43 *Personification of Hope. Stucco group in the rotunda, personally made by Christian Wenzinger.*

zerland began shortly after his death in 1487, although it was only in 1669 that he was beatified and only in 1947 canonized. Next to him is the ascetic *Johannes Kalybita*[6], venerated in the East, who lived in his parents' house as an unidentified servant until his death, a similar fate to that of *Alexius of Edessa*[7], who appears to the right of the balustrade. BEATI MITES (Blessed are the meek, Matt. 5,5). At the top of this group is *Francis of Sales* (1567–1622)[8], Bishof of Geneva, with seat in Annecy, founder of the Order of the Nuns of the Visitation. The burning heart entwined with thorns refers to the renewer of the Catholic faith in the Savoyard Chablais. The monk below him is *John Gualbert*[9], a Florentine Reform Benedictine monk of the 11th century and founder of the Vallombrosa Order. The two figures to his left are *King David*[10] with a harp, ancestor of Christ, and *Moses*[11] with the tablets of the Ten Commandments, author of the Old Testament dispensation, which was reformed by Jesus. The Benedictine with the broken staff is the poet-monk *Notker the Stammerer* (d. 912)[12], venerated in St.Gall as a saint, who broke his staff in combat with the Devil. The kneeling woman on the left with the widow's veil, over whose head Notker extends his staff, is *Monica*[13], the mother of St.Augustine. Next to her, with the crown, is *Elizabeth of Thueringia*[14], daughter of King Andrew II of Hungary, a benefactress who was canonized in 1235. BEATI QUI LUGENT (Blessed are they who mourn). The Benedictine with the two eyeballs in his left hand is the monk *Victor*[15], who was blinded outside the monastery and ended his days in 960 on the Viktorsberg, named after him, in the Vorarlberg. To his left, in a white dress, sits *St.Bruno*[16], with a cross, the founder of the Carthusian order. The mitre at his feet refers to his refusal to take up the seat of bishop of Reims. To the right of Victor we see the penitent *Mary Magdalene*[17], with lifted hands and flowing hair. Down at the border of the cupola is *Mary the Egyptian*[18], who began as a harlot and finished her life as an anchorite in the desert. Another repentant sinner is the thief who was crucified at the right hand of Christ and was later included among the saints as *St.Dismas*[19]. BEATI QUI ESURIUNT ET SITIUNT IUSTITIAM (Blessed are they who hunger and thirst after righteousness). The crowning figure of a monk is that of the Father Abbot *Benedict of Nursia* (480–547)[20] with the attribute of a poison beaker: to the right, pointing to him, the Dominican *Thomas Aquinus* (ca.1225–1274)[21]. The putto with a book refers to his major work «Summa Theologica». Following, on the left, is *Ignatius Loyola* (1491–1556)[22], founder of the Jesuit order. He wears a liturgical vestment with a christogram as a sign of his devotion to Christ (the Jesuit arms). Next to him on the left, *Bonaventure of Bagnoreggio* (ca. 1217–1274)[23]. He was general minister of the Franciscans, a cardinal and an important theologian. Left, below him, *Anthony the Hermit*[24], with an angel bringing him the cross with small bells. BEATI MISERICORDES (Blessed are the merciful). At the very top, *Charles Borromeo* (1538–1584)[25], the great Milanese cardinal and reformer of the Catholic Church who visited St.Gall in 1570 (see the Charles Borromeo Gate, p.195). The figure of the old man on the right is very probably that of the Old Testament prophet *Tobias*[26]. For once he is not depicted with his accompanying angel, but with a shovel, representing him as a gravedigger (the gift of mercy). Below, in ermine, the French *King Louis IX*[27] (reigned 1226–1270), the saint who built the Sainte-Chapelle in Paris and organized two crusades. The Benedictine next to him is probably Abbot *Purchart* (ruled 1001–1021)[28], who restored monastic discipline at St.Gall and was later greatly venerated. According to Jansen, the figure of a woman between them is *Martha*[29], the «hostess of Christ». The seated bishop at the border of the cupola is *Martin of Tours* (d. 397)[30], a French missionary and patron saint of the French kings. BEATI MUNDO CORDE (Blessed are the pure in heart). At the top, *Scholastica*[31] with a small dove, to remind us that her brother Benedict saw her soul floating up to Heaven in the form of a dove. The Benedictine with a lily is the hermit *Gerold*[32], who gave his goods to the monastery of Einsiedeln and sent two of his sons to the same monastery (an unusual representation of him). Next to him on the left we see *Catharine of Alexandria*[33], easily recognizable by her broken wheel. On the other side, above a picture of the church, *Emperor Heinrich II* (reigned 1002–1024)[34], who endowed the cathedral of Bamberg and who is buried there. Below him, his spouse *Kunigunde* (d. 1033)[35], who was canonized in 1200. BEATI PACIFICI (Blessed are the peacemakers). The top figure of a monk, according to Jansen, is a Pope Clement. This might be *Clement II* (reigned 1046–1047)[36], the restorer of the papacy. However, there is no papal attribute. It may also be an homage to the pope reigning at the time the cupola was painted, Pope Clement XIII (reigned 1758–1769). Below him we see *Pope Leo I, the Great* (reigned 440–461)[37], who saved Rome from the invasion of the Huns. Opposite him sits Bishop *Ulrich of Augsburg* (reigned 923–963)[38], who was much involved in the victory of the Christians over the Huns in 955 on the Lechfeld (F.R.G.). The fish attribute refers to the miracle in which a piece of meat was transformed into a fish on Friday. Between the two prelates sits *Bernard of Clairvaux* (1090–1153)[39], founder of the Cistercian order and a great mystic. To the left of this group of saints sits a queen, said to be *Elizabeth of Portugal* (d. 1336)[40]. She was a great-niece of the above-mentioned Elizabeth of Thueringia and she too was known for her acts of charity. The half figure next to her is the patriarch and Greek Father of the Church *Cyrill of Alexandria*[41], identifiable by his pallium with a small cross. BEATI QUI PERSECUTIONEM PATIUNTUR (Blessed are those who are persecuted for righteousness' sake). The top female figure with a chalice and tower is *Barbara*[42]. Left, next to her, shown as a nun, is *Idda of Toggenburg*[43] with a deer; the lights in its antlers are said

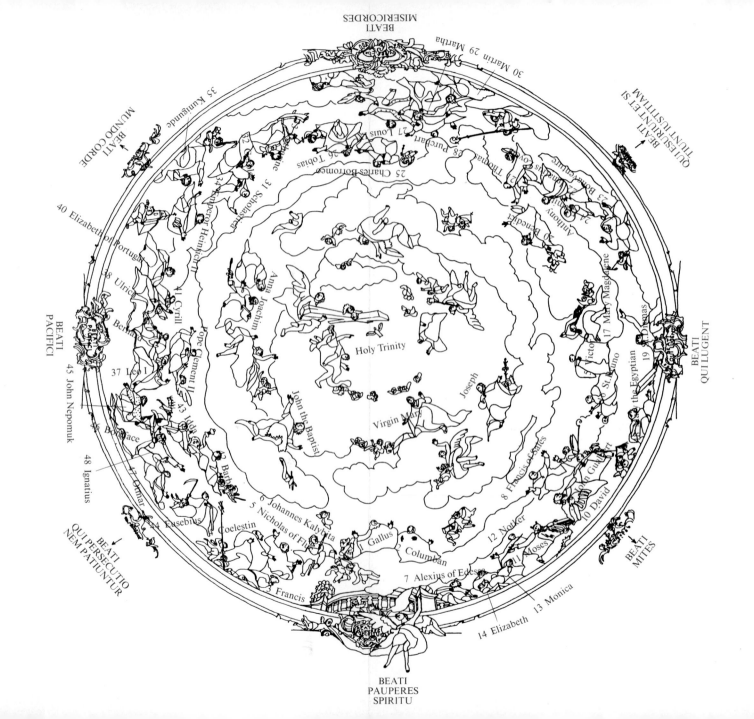

to have lit her way in Fischingen. The figure of the monk *Eusebius*[44] with a scythe, alluding to his martyrdom, is characteristic. His small monastery on the Viktorsberg at Feldkirch became part of the monastery of St.Gall in 882, where Eusebius was subsequently venerated as a local saint. On the outside left we see *John Nepomuk*[45] of Prague, with an ermine-trimmed stole, indicating him to be the representative of higher spirituality. The martyr's palm refers to the fact that he was drowned in the Moldau river in 1393 because he refused to betray the secrecy of the confessional. The large figure of a bishop at whose feet lies a book pierced with a sword must be *Boniface*[46], the great folk apostle of Germany, who was murdered in 754. The seated monk with pluvial and wine cask is *Otmar*[47], the first abbot of St.Gall. The figure of the old man with the white beard is that of the bishop and martyr *Ignatius Theophorus of Antioch*[48], who is greatly revered in the Eastern Church. *Fides,* mentioned by Jansen, cannot be found. Since he mentions that this painting was restored in 1773, it may be that a saint painted subsequently was lost during the uncovering restoration of 1966.

The *stucco figures* below the dome are the work of CHRISTIAN WENZINGER himself. In the large pendentives above the pilasters of the choir and of the nave monumental personifications of the *principal virtues* rise out of the clouds: Faith with chalice and cross, Hope with an anchor, Love of God with tongue of fire and Charity with children; in the smaller pendentives, groups of putti with allegories of virtue: south, Justice with sword and scales, and Moderation with beaker and glass; north, Strength with tamed lion, and Wisdom with serpent rod and mirror.

Sides of the cupola
5a. IN DEFENSIONEM EVANGELII (For the defence of the Gospel, Phil. 1,17). St.Gallus is shown the map of the region of Toggenburg, which had been under the rule

of the monastery of St.Gall since 1468. Above this we see Idda, countess and patroness of Toggenburg with a deer. Right, the saint of the catacombs Marinus, in Lichtensteig (his bones were transferred in 1657) and Leander at the convent of Wattwil (1652). On the wall tablets are stucco groups: left, with the Toggenburg flag and sword, right, with drum and trumpet.

5b. IN DEFENSIONEM EVANGELII (For the defence of the Gospel). The text from the Epistle of St.Paul to the Philippians (1,16) refers to Christians in prison for their faith (allusion to the martyrs). St.Gallus blesses the Old Territory of St.Gall which an angel shows him on a map. Surrounding Gallus are four saints of the catacombs venerated in this country: above, Honoratus and Antonius, whose bones were transferred in 1643 and 1653 respectively, to the abbey church of St.Gall; below, Justinus in Gossau (1743) and Pankratius in Wil (1672) with palm branches and laurel wreaths. On the wall tablets, groups of putti: left, bearer on the escutcheon of the monastery of St.Gall (a bear on its coat of arms), with drummer and trumpeter; right, bearer of the St.Gall banners and sword, the symbols in both cases of the worldly power of the prince-abbot.

5c. GRATIA SANITATUM (Gifts of healing, I. Cor. 12,9). The ceiling painting has been almost entirely renewed. In the centre we see St.Valentine, Bishop of Terni, with an epileptic child lying at his feet. In St.Gall there existed a St.Valentine brotherhood which was much loved by the people. Left, St.Sebastian with an arrow, then the saints of the catacombs Sergius and Bacchus, Hiacynthus and Erasmus, who cannot be individually distinguished; their bones were all transferred to the abbey church of St.Gall in 1680. The ceremonies are shown in a copper engraving in the Library. On the wall tablets: left, two putti with votive gifts in the form of infants in swaddling clothes; right, two putti with a chain of various votive gifts.

76

44 Group of putti in stucco, in a side space of the southern part of the rotunda, based on a design by Christian Wenzinger.

5d. FORTITUDO ET DECOR (Strength and orna- ⁴⁵
ment). In the centre we see, floating on a cloud, the
Mother of God with a sceptre, as Queen of Heaven; on
the right, St.Catherine and St.Dominicus receive a garland of roses; on the left, the Carmelites Theresa of Avila
(1515–1582) and Simon Stock (d. 1265) accept the scapular. The superior of the order, who died in Bordeaux,
was known for his vision of the scapular. On the wall tablets; left, two putti with a wreath of roses, right, with a

scapular, referring respectively to the ceiling painting of the Rosary brotherhood (1636), and to the Scapular brotherhood (1733).

5e. AD PROFECTUM EVANGELII (To spread the Gospel, Phil. 1,7). An angel presents to St.Gallus the coat of arms of the provincial chapter of St.Gall (red patriarchal cross on a blue field). On the left, with cardinal's insignia, is St.Charles Borromeo (d. 1584), who came to be particularly revered at St.Gall after his visit in 1570 (see Charles Borromeo Gate, p.197); right, Bishop Conrad of Constance (d. 976), patron of the diocese of Constance, with a chalice and a spider. Below, the saint of the catacombs Theodore, at the monastery of Neu St.Johann (his bones were ceremonially transferred there in 1685) and Benedict at the convent of St.Scholastica in Rorschach (1732). On the wall tablets: left, three putti with a missal and stole, right, two putti with small mass bells, book and biretta.

5f. AD PROFECTUM EVANGELII (To spread the Gospel, Phil. 1,7). St.Gallus asks for a blessing for the rural chapter of Wil; its coat of arms (Good Shepherd on a blue field) is presented by an angel. Left, the Roman martyr Laureatus in Wildhaus (bones transferred in 1676); right, St.Elizabeth of Thueringia and Gebhard, Bishop of Constance (reigned 979–995), founder of the Abbey of Petershausen. The tiara on the right refers to the transfer of the headquarters of Pope Gregory the Great to Constance. On the wall plates, groups of putti: left, with a stole, chalice and book; right, with a pluvial, censer, incense boat and processional cross.

The choir

6. In the centre bay we see the Lamb of God on the book with seven seals, surrounded by putti, surmounted by the Christogram IHS in a gloriole. At the border angels float carrying the instruments of the Passion of Christ; clockwise: cross, chain, lantern, nails, dice, whipping-post,

45 *Mary bestows the Rosary and Scapular brotherhood on Katharina and Dominikus, and Theresia and Simon Stock, respectively. South bay of the rotunda.*

46 *The four Greek Fathers of the Church in typical pontifical garb of the Orthodox Church. First south bay of the choir.*

whip, crown of thorns, rooster, Judas' bag, lance and hyssop rod. The inscription «CONTINET HOC SANCTUM SANCTORUM MILLIA TEMPLUM» on the western transverse arch relates to the cupola.

6a. ADMIRABILIS (Admirable). Below the cloud-bordered eye of God sit the four Latin Fathers of the Church (see also their individual representations in the Library, p.104ff.); from left to right: Archbishop Ambrosius of Milan with a quill and book, Pope Gregory the Great in pontifical robes with the dove of the Holy Spirit, accompanied by an angel with a ferula (papal staff) and scroll inscribed «Regina Coeli» (Queen of Heaven – the beginning of an antiphony to the Blessed Virgin written by Gregory); Bishop Augustinus of Hippo with a book and pen, accompanied by an angel with a ladle (the study of the Trinity is as difficult as emptying the ocean with a ladle); Jerome in the desert in penitent's garb with lions and a celestial trumpet. Above the pilaster capital, two putti with the inscription «LIBER GENERATIONIS JESU CHRISTI F. David» (Lineage of Jesus Christ, the son of David, Matthew 1,1).

㊻ 6b. PRINCEPS PACIS (Prince of peace). Below the symbol of the Trinity, three interlaced rings, the four Greek Fathers of the Church, dressed in the pontifical robes of the Eastern Church, are seated on clouds. All wear the mandyas (pluvial) and the omophorion (pallium) and are distinguished by their crown and paterissa (crosier) as ecclesiastical dignitaries. The figures cannot be identified individually. The sequence according to Jansen is: Athanasius the Great, Basil the Great, Gregory of Nazianzus and John Chrysostomus (see their individual representations in the Library, p.108ff.). Above the capital, putti with a scroll inscribed «SANCTUS, SANCTUS, SANCTUS» (Holy, holy, holy).

7. LAUDENT NOMEN EIUS IN CHORO (Praise His name in the congregation). In clouds, with putti and two seraphim the name Jahveh is written in Hebrew let-

ters. On an intermediate plane, the Mother of God with a halo and crescent moon, a serpent at her feet (the Immaculate Conception) and open arms. To her left, according to Jansen, Zachary and Elizabeth, as well as the old man Simeon in priest's robe; right, King David with a crown and harp, and Moses with the Tablets of the Law, accompanied by three other prophets. Below, an angel standing before a flight of steps recommends a kneeling cleric to St.Benedict. The latter points to the end of his nineteenth rule: «Concordet S. Reg. cap. XIX» (. . . that our thoughts and our heart be in accordance with our voice). The book is held by an angel. On the step, left, below the lattice is the signature of the painter of the frescoes: «Josephus Wannenmacher inv . . .».

7a. CONSILIARIUS (Counsellor). The four archangels are depicted; from left to right: Raphael with a walking staff, referring to his accompanying the young Tobias (the distorted face that appears below him may also refer to help at the Last Judgement, but in that case, the archangel would more likely be Uriel); Gabriel with a lily, the announcer of the Word of God to Mary; Michael with a sword as conqueror of Lucifer and scales as the weigher of souls at the Last Judgement, Uriel (?) with a censer, who accompanies the dead to judgement. Above the capital, putti with a scroll inscribed «SANCTUS, SANCTUS, SANCTUS, SANCTUS».

7b. PATER FUTURI SAECULI (The Father of the world to come). Angel choir: on the left, a guardian angel embraces a monk; in the centre two violin players; on the right, an angel with viola da gamba and two additional small angels holding sheets of music. The relationship with the choir organ is evident. Above the capital, putti with a scroll inscribed «Cum baptizati CHRISTO estis Paulus» (For as baptized in Christ you have put on Christ, Gal. 3,27).

8. EMANUEL nobiscum DEUS (God, Emanuel, is with us). In the centre Christ stands with a chalice on the

terrestrial globe, surrounded by angels. Above him, the
Sacred Heart with a crown of thorns in a gloriole, encircled by putti and two worshipping angels. Below, the
four Evangelists: left, Mark with a lion and Matthew
with an angel; right, Luke with a bull and John with an
eagle. The attributes refer on the one hand to the authors
of the individual gospels, and on the other to the apoca-
lyptic tetramorph. At the top of the arch of the apse is a
clock in stucco rocaille.

8a. DEUS (God). Six apostles. In the middle Peter
sits on a cross, which refers to his martyrdom, holding
keys and a scourge, symbols of his mission and of his
penance for his betrayal of Christ; the domed building
behind him refers to St.Peter's in Rome (see the representation of the Church in the Library, p.107); left, Andrew with his cross, James the Elder with a pilgrim's
staff and pouch, and a sword; in the background, Paul
with a sword; right Thomas with a lance and James the
Younger with a rod. On the pilaster capital is the insrip-
tion «NIMIS CONFORTATUS PRINCIPATUS EO-
RUM» (Great is the glory of the Lord, Psalm 138).

8b. FORTIS (Powerful). The other six apostles: from
left to right: Simon with a saw, Barnabas (honorary apostle) with a stone, Bartholomew with flayed skin, Philip
with a cross, Matthew with an axe, Judas Thaddeus with
a mathematical square and a club. Above the capital is
the inscription «NIMIS EXALTATUS ES SUPER
OMNES DEOS» Psalm 96 (For you are raised above all
gods).

9. Dome of the apse. The inside of the dome,
painted by JOSEF KELLER as recently as 1809/10, shows
an angel choir, with God the Father above as creator of
the world. The painting differs from the Wannenmacher
frescoes by its more colourful palette.

9a. Burning Heart of Mary, entwined with roses and
pierced by a sword, in a gloriole, surrounded by clouds,
with putti.

82

9b. Rose-entwined heart with verdant staff of St.Joseph, surrounded by clouds, with putti.

The short inscriptions found in the side aisles of the choir, reading from left (starting at the rear) to right (starting at the front), are a Scripture passage from Isaiah 9,6, included in the introit of the first mass on Christmas Day: (ET VOCABITUR NOMEN EIUS) ADMIRABILIS CONSILIARIUS DEUS FORTIS PATER FUTURI SAECULI PRINCEPS PACIS (And His name will be Wonderful, Counsellor, the mighty God, the everlasting Father, the Prince of Peace).

47 Christ as the founder of the New Testament. Ceiling painting in the first bay of the choir. Paintings in the apse, 1809/10, by Josef Keller.

The Monastery Buildings

Since the earliest times there was a cloister surrounded by monastic buildings to the south of the abbey church. It can be seen on the plan for the monastery of St.Gall of about 820/30. The architectural stages of the cloister in the Middle Ages are difficult to identify because of the lack of sources. The changes which took place, particularly during the 16th century, are demonstrated by rather fortuitous finds of pieces of architectural sculpture. The sculpted keystones preserved in the Lapidarium (p.127) suggest a cloister-walk with a Gothic ribbed vault perhaps similar to that in Mariaberg in Rorschach. In 1551 the west wing was rebuilt as a library. On the south side stood – somewhat to the west of the centre – the hospital, which also appears to have been built in the middle of the 16th century, and survived until 1758. Only the east wing appears to have consisted largely of old components, before it was destroyed in 1674 and rebuilt from the ground up. Diagonally across from the east wing stood the old palace, the official and private residence of the abbot, which was relocated here by Abbot Diethelm Blarer (ruled 1530–1564) and in 1666 gave way to the present Baroque palace wing.

The «Ichnographia» of Father GABRIEL HECHT of 1719 indicates the purpose of the individual monastic buildings and of the adjoining annexes on the south side. Under Prince-Abbot Coelestin Gugger von Staudach the monastery quadrangle was rebuilt, with the exception of the eastern section, as it still appears today. Its Baroque unity can be seen particularly well in the rib-vaulted cloister-walk, which encloses the entire inner courtyard and also skirts the rotunda of the cathedral. The east wing with the monks' cells was raised by one storey and crowned with a small belfry.

The Library in the West Wing

Architectural history

The first real library building, built during the time of Abbot Diethelm Blarer (1551/52) made up – together with the archives – the west wing of the then smaller monastery quadrangle to the south side of the church (see Late Gothic keystones on p.127 and positional diagram on p.19). In 1758 Abbot Coelestin Gugger von Staudach had the west and south wings demolished and rebuilt. To build the library section, which had been displaced somewhat further westwards, he employed the aged PETER THUMB, who was already working on the abbey church, and his son, MICHAEL PETER. After only six months the library building was already roofed. The internal wood fittings were produced in the monastery workshop under the direction of Brother GABRIEL LOSER. The ceiling paintings, dated 1762, carry the signature of JOSEF WANNENMACHER, who had painted the nave and rotunda of the abbey church. The stucco work was executed by the well-known GIGL Brothers. The furniture, particularly in the manuscript room, was completed during the time of Abbot Beda Angehrn (ruled 1767–1796).

In contrast to most famous monastic libraries, the room not only remained largely untouched, despite the dissolution of the monastery in 1805, but the collection of manuscripts, incunabula and books it housed remained almost undisturbed. Restorations took place, in particular in 1934 (ceiling paintings) and 1954 when the top storey was made fireproof. In 1950 the former residence of the librarian was converted into offices and a fine reading room.

Description

The Library takes up the second and third floors of the west wing, without any indication of this from the outside. Access is through the stairwell in the central projection of the south wing. On the second floor, a door with the carved arms of Abbot Beda Angehrn affixed to its inner side allows entry.

In the corridor we are greeted first of all by a series of emblematic *typological pictures* with the arms and laudatory texts relating to a total of eight post-Reform abbots, from Kilian Germann (ruled 1529–1530) to Josephus von Rudolphi (1717–1740). However, Abbots Otmar Kunz and Leodegar Buergisser are missing. Above is an emblem, accompanied by scenes from the Old Testament which are related to the incumbency of the relevant abbot; in the centre, the arms of the abbot; below, an accompanying Latin text giving details and dates; at the sides are small pictures with commentaries. The series, whose form is based on the tablets eulogizing Swiss Benedictine monasteries in the east wing (p.137), was produced during the time of Abbot Coelestin (ruled 1740–1767). We know this because an allegorical painting with a related theme (no. 9) bears the date 1741 and the signature *«Carl Anton Weber»*. It is questionable whether this otherwise unknown artist was also involved in the production of the abbey paintings, since the latter show, in the frame surmounts,

48 *South-west view of the ecclesiastical buildings. The Library takes up the second and third storeys.*

86

unequivocally Rococo style elements which point to a time later than the middle of the 18th century. Certain characteristics of style and motive, and the brisk, nervous way of painting with light-dark contrasts and white highlights suggest that JOSEF WANNENMACHER is the artist.

1. KILLIANUS ZELOSUS. Abbot Kilian Germann (ruled 1529–1530), «the Zealous». In the top picture, a landscape with setting sun: «Dum ardet occidit» (That which burns, sinks), probably in reference to the flight of the monastic community from St.Gall during the troubles of the Reformation. Left, the heathen idol which was destroyed by Judas Maccabeus (Macc. 45); right, two generals reach out towards each other. Six small framed pictures, the one on the right depicting the accidental death of the Abbot in the Bregenz river.

2. DIETHELM MAGNANIMUS. Abbot Diethelm Blarer of Wartensee (ruled 1530–1564), «the Magnanimous». The top picture shows Noah's Ark and the dove: «Optatae Pacis Nuntia» (The messenger of the ardently desired peace), in remembrance of the return of the abbot and the revitalization of the monastery after the Reformation. Left: Joshua orders the sun to stand still (Jos. 10,12); right: return of the Ark of the Covenant to Jerusalem under King Solomon (1 Kings 8,1). In the medallion below, left, we see the library wing built by Abbot Diethelm (ruled 1551/53).

3. JOACHIMUS RELIGIOSUS. Abbot Joachim Opser (ruled 1577–1594), «the Pious». A pelican is depicted plucking open its own breast in order to feed its young with its blood: «Pio Amoris Vulnere» (Through the wound of love pleasing to God). Left: King Ezechias has the brazen serpent destroyed (2 Kings 18,4); right, an angel appears to Joshua as a comrade in battle at Jericho (Jos. 5,13). The small picture at the top right shows lightning striking the tower of the abbey church in 1588, and the seven bells; lower right, the death of the abbot in the pulpit.

4. BERNARDUS MAGNUS. Abbot Bernhard Mueller (ruled 1594–1630), «the Great». The beehive is a reference to his patron St.Bernard, whose speech flowed like honey: «Congregat et regit» (He gathers together and reigns), a reference to the Swiss Benedictine congregation established by Abbot Bernhard. Since Abbot Bernhard is referred to in the text as «novus Esdras», we see, on the left, Esdras (Ezra), teaching the laws of Moses, and right, the scourging of Mischah (1 Ezra 9,7). Lower right, medallion with a view of the abbey church as it appeared in the early 17th century, and the construction of the new Otmar church, in 1623.

5. PIUS VERE PIUS. Abbot Pius Reher (ruled 1630–1654), «the Truly Pious». Representation of a lily in front of a mirror: «Recipit et Refert» (He receives and gives back). The lily refers to the Rosary brotherhoods introduced during the time of Abbot Pius Reher. Left: King Josiah has the Book of the Covenant read to him (3 Kings 23,2) and the Passover celebrated (2 Kings 23,21). Abbot Pius promoted education, built a new high altar in the abbey church, and introduced the art of printing in Neu St.Johann in 1641.

6. GALLUS GLORIOSUS. Abbot Gallus Alt (ruled 1654–1687), «the Glorious». The picture shows a rooster, the heraldic animal of the abbot, between two vineyards: «Foecunda & Venusta» (Fruitful and lovable). Left: Gideon kneels before the dewy fleece (Judges 6,37); right: the Israelites lapping water in Gideon's army fighting the Midianites (Judges 7,5). In a small picture in the margin on the right we see the east wing of the monastery, which he built in 1674. Below, on the left, he receives the Order of the Annunciation from allied Savoy in 1686.

7. COELESTINUS I. SAPIENS. Abbot and Cardinal Coelestin I. Sfondrati (ruled 1687–1696), «the Wise». Arms with a cardinal's hat. The picture shows the Tower of David festooned with martial emblems: «Om-

nis armatura fortium» (All the arms for the strong). The erudition and wisdom of the abbot are especially praised: he is compared with King Solomon. Solomon is seen on the left next to the emblem; on the right he is seen writing down the Song of Songs.

8. JOSEPHUS CLEMENS. Abbot Josephus von Rudolphi (ruled 1717–1740), «the Gentle». The sun above a field of wheat: «Redit ut foecundet» (It returns, in order to fructify), a reference to the new impetus given to the monastery after the Peace of Baden. The years of his incumbency are compared with the seven fruitful years in Egypt. Left: Pharaoh appoints Joseph to the position of minister (Gen. 41); right: Joseph receives his brothers (Gen. 45).

9. *Allegorical picture.* This painting, unusual from the ⑭⑨ iconographic point of view, is a theological allegory of the monastery of St.Gall. In the bottom right-hand corner is the signature of the artist: Carl Anton Weber, 1741. At the top, the inscription «DUODENA BENEDICTIO COELESTIS IN MONASTERIUM S. GALLI PER DUODECIM SAECULA» (A twelve-fold heavenly blessing on the monastery of St.Gall for twelve centuries). On the left, a chariot with the symbols of the four Evangelists carries a woman on whom the sun shines, the embodiment of the New Testament. Right, Elias going up to Heaven, a prefiguration of Christ. The woman sitting in the centre, with the globe and sceptre of the Trinity, personifies divine Providence. In the middle, in a purple tent between the columns, sits a woman in priestly robes, with a chalice, host, cross and tiara, as the personification of the Catholic Church. Above the canopy are the crossed keys and tiara of the papal symbols. On the scroll: «MULTA GLORIAM FECIT MAGNIFICENTIA SUA A SAECULO (Eccl. 44 V.2)» (Much glory has the Highest given you over the centuries). Above the columns float three angels with shields which read, left: «PER SUMMOS PRINCIPES CONSTANTER CONSERVATA» (Always protected by the

greatest princes); in the centre: «PER SUMMOS PONTI-FICES COPIOSE DERIVATA» (By the popes richly endowed); right: «PER PROPRIOS ABBATES FELICITER PROPAGATA» (By their own abbots felicitously promoted). Among the columns on the left are the representatives of worldly power: «HOMINES MAGNI VIRTUTE» (Men great in virtue), followed by a king and an emperor: «DOMINANTES IN POTESTATIBUS» (Rulers with authority); on the right, among the columns, the figures of Gallus and Otmar standing alone. The scroll above them reads: «LAUDAMUS VIROS GLORIOSOS ET PARENTES NOSTROS» (We praise the glorious men and our ancestors). In front of them, three saints of St.Gall, Magnus, Notker and Eusebius, with the inscription «IN GENERATIONE SUA» (In their generation). On the entablature, six coats of arms, relating to the personages below; left: imaginary arms of the Confederation, French royal arms and arms of the German Empire; right, from front to back: arms of the monastery of St.Gall, and imaginary arms of Otmar and Gallus. At the sides of the tent, two emblems: left, Noah's Ark with a scroll: «Refugium nobis a Generatione in Generatione» (Our refuge from generation to generation); right, Gideon's fleece: «Pluviae Benedictionis erunt» (The dew of blessing shall be upon you [the Church]). The six symbolic pictures on the plinth refer to the figures above; a tower festooned with arms: «Omnis Armature Fortium» (All arms for the strong); a warrior: «Ne movearis» (You shall not yield); an eagle in combat with snakes: «Protegar in Velamento Alarum Tuarum» (I seek protection under your wing); right: a hand with bread: «Ego Plantavi» (I have planted); a hand with a water container: «Ego Rigavi» (I have watered); the rain of manna: «Deus Incrementum dedit» (God has given fruit). At the foot of the canopy sit putti, personifying three callings: the soldier with helmet, sword and booty, the teacher with key and a container from which he is pouring, and a farmer, with a hat, shovel and cornucopia. In each of the lower corners sit three unidentified female saints with laurel wreaths; between these two groups is a very exact bird's eye view of the monastery of St.Gall at the time of the great architectural changes of the Late Baroque period.

49 *Allegorical picture of the Monastery of St.Gall, 1741, by Carl Anton Weber. In the Library.*

At the western end of the corridor is an impressive *doorway flanked by columns* in grey and black imitation marble, perhaps the work of FRANZ ANTON DIRR in 1781. Over the door panels is a resplendent Rococo Cartouche bearing the Greek inscription *ΨΥΧΗΣ ΙΑΤΡΕΙΟΝ*, which, freely translated, means «the sanatorium of the soul» or «the soul's pharmacy». A putto at each side bids the visitor welcome.

50 *Door to the Library, probably by Franz Anton Dirr, 1781.*

The room we enter gives an impression of surprising intimacy and radiance. The extremely rich *natural wood furnishings,* the book spines and the extensively painted stucco ceiling draw attention away from the well-proportioned, four-sectioned hall with wall pilasters. All the decoration is in motion, flooded by light from the fifteen windows. The *curve of the gallery,* which rests on projecting columns, is a characteristic feature of the room. The upper storey, with a railing with wide openings, appears to float. The walls and pilasters are totally masked by books, and create an awe-inspiring ecclesiastical atmosphere. The *floor* is inlaid with four large stars and intertwined loops in walnut. Each of the short sides has a door to the gallery (the northern one now leads to the lift for the book stacks). Above the northern door the carved arms of Abbot Coelestin II, who was responsible for the construction, are surmounted by his portrait, by JOSEF WANNENMACHER, 1766. Above the gallery door hangs a picture of St.Cecilia, bought in 1602 by Father Jodok Metzler (1574–1639) in Rome for Abbot Bernhard Mueller. This copy, based on an original by the Ticino painter STEFANO MADERNO, shows the dead martyr as she is said to have been found in 1599 in the sarcophagus of St.Cecilia in Trastevere, during the time of Cardinal Paolo Camillo Sfondrati (1561–1618). The painting subsequently had a direct link with St.Gall, because the nephew of Sfondrati, Abbot Coelestin Sfondrati, became titular bishop of this Roman church on being made a cardinal himself, and was laid to rest there in 1696. Only the heart of this prince of the Church was returned to St.Gall and is entombed in the abbey church (see p.45).

On the opposite side, a hidden spiral staircase leads to the gallery and to the scriptorium. Above the door hangs the portrait of Abbot Beda Angehrn, flanked by two putti with the abbot's insignia. In the lunette above the entrance to the Manuscript Room there is a long,

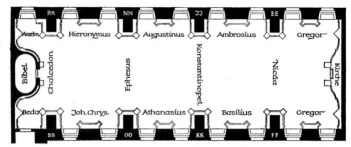

51 Plan of the Library ceiling, with indications of the painting subjects and of the book classifications in the gallery.

stretched-out painting showing Christ entombed, an outstanding copy of the famous picture by Hans Holbein the Younger in the public art collection of Basle, acquired second-hand in 1724 by Abbot Josephus von Rudolphi.

Particularly noteworthy are *20 putti* measuring approximately 31 to 34 cm in height, which are hardly noticeable in the decoration as a whole but have artistic and iconographic charm. They stand in niches above the pilasters in the window recesses, as well as at the narrow sides. They represent the arts, sciences and crafts, but do not relate to the content of the books in their vicinity. In any case, the present arrangement of the books is not the original one. Our listing follows the alphabet of the library. A: The poet. B: The physician. C: The botanist

52 Floor plan of the marquetry work in the Library.

53 Library, built in 1758 by Peter Thumb, woodwork by Brother Gabriel Loser. View to the north.

and the carpenter. D: The pharmacist and the bell caster. E: The gun maker and the goldsmith. H: The flautist and the singer. L: The painter and the gardener. M: The composer and the merchant. P: The sculptor and the geographer. Q: The architect and the astronomer. T: The mathematician. U: The organ builder. These charming little figures are in the style of CHRISTIAN WENZINGER, who was even named as their sculptor by the later librarian and member of the monastic community, Brother Franz Weidemann (1774–1843). They are indeed very similar in style to the stucco putti in the rotunda of the abbey church, even though the possibility of their being the work of the sculptors FRANZ ANTON DIRR, JOSEF SCHWAIGER or FIDEL SPORER cannot be excluded. Whether these little figures were originally planned for the Library is questionable. There are nine comparable pairs of statuettes of children, each only 12 cm high, in the panelled room of the Baronenhaus in Wil; they also

95

54 The astronomer and the architect. Two putti in the Library, from the workshop of Christian Wenzinger.

represent individual professions but are not in colour. The small format suggests, in both cases, that the figures may have served as models for the stucco worker; those at St.Gall may only subsequently have found a place of honour in the Library. In addition to the *Carolingian monastery plan,* there is also on permanent exhibition a *Baroque model of the abbey of St.Gall,* which was made by Brother GABRIEL LOSER, a member of the community, in 1751/52. This is an original interpretation of the plans of JOHANN CASPAR BAGNATO and may be considered as the direct preliminary phase of the project carried out by PETER THUMB. The Egyptian mummy is a curiosity and has been in the Library since the 19th century.

The Ceiling Paintings

The shallow plaster vault pierced almost to the centre by lunettes in the window axes has four large paintings rich

96

in figures, with bold trompe-l'œil perspectives and accompanying cartouches. The parts of the vault not covered by paintings have large-scale *rococo stucco work,* in places detached, in delicate tones of red on a greenish ground, made in 1761 by the brothers JOHANN GEORG and MATHIAS GIGL of Wessobrunn. With the exception of two roosters, which appear near gallery book-cases KK and TT and may be the distinctive mark of the GIGL brothers (Gueggel means «rooster» in Swiss German), the stucco is purely decorative and is only in isolated places interwoven with floral elements and architectural set pieces. The stucco work shoots out boldly over the edges of the painted surfaces.

Despite their dark, almost gloomy, colours, the *ceiling paintings* by JOSEF WANNENMACHER are a grandiose depiction of the first four Councils of Christendom. Hosts of ecclesiastical dignitaries move in Utopian halls with bold architectural perspectives. Individuals and groups engage in animated debate on the nature of the heavenly persons, for example the Virgin Mary, who appear in a cloud-lined sky and take an active part in the discussion. Wannenmacher paints as matter-of-factly as if his work were based on generally known earlier paintings. However, to our knowledge, this theme has never been represented in such a monumental way either before or after him. Even though the iconographic treatment is related to numerous representations of the Council of Trent, the individual treatment of the main characters, the costumes of the Roman and Greek dignitaries and the visualization of the theological ideas are astonishing. The artist allows the erudite instructions of his patron to flow effortlessly into the composition, and reveals himself as a first-class painter.

The Council of Nicaea in the year 325   ⑤⑤

At the bottom of the painting is a cartouche with the inscription «NON PRAEVALEBUNT. Matth. 16 V. 18».

The text is taken from the Gospel according to St.Matthew: «And I tell you, you are Peter and on this rock will I build my church, and the powers of death shall not prevail against it.» In terms of content the text belongs rather to the representation of the Church above the gallery (p.107), but can also relate to the first Council, where the orthodoxy of the Roman Church was defined. In the year 325 the Emperor Constantine the Great (reigned 306–337) summoned the bishops to Nicaea to the first general Council, in order to settle the Arian controversy. The Bishop of Rome at that time was Pope Sylvester I (reigned 314–335). The venue was the imperial summer palace, which the painter includes in the scene as a Baroque architectural background with archways. Above the balustrade the Emperor is shown sending out the bishops. In the central niche is a canopied throne, on which lies a book with the beginning of the Gospel according to St.John: «IN PRINCIPIO ERAT VERBUM Joan Cap. 1» (In the beginning was the Word). To the right of this sits the Emperor Constantine. The discussion of the approximately 300 bishops gathered together from West and East is concerned with St.John's concept of the Logos (Word), which postulates the intrinsic divinity of all three persons (Trinity). Arius, a priest of Alexandria, and a large number of followers denied the divinity of Christ. Arianism endangered not only the unity of the Roman Church, but also that of the Roman Empire. Arius himself appears to the left of the centre, with imploring gestures, accompanied by two bishops who point to the word «$ANOMOIO\Sigma$» (Non-consubstantial). In his opinion Christ was created by the Father, but is another and not identical with Him, a being created from the void, and fallible by nature. Bishop Ossius of Córdoba sits on the canopied throne on the left facing the followers of Arius, surrounded by two cardinals and by priests and deacons. As the representative of Pope Sylvester I and the West, he holds a scroll with the Latin concept

55 *The Council of Nicaea. Ceiling painting in the Library, signed by Josef Wannenmacher, 1762.*

«CONSUBSTANTIALIS» (Christ consubstantial with the Father), which was subsequently included in the Nicene Creed: «GENITUM NON FACTUM, CONSUBSTANTIALEM PATRI» (Begotten, not created, one in being with the Father). To strengthen this principle of orthodoxy, an angel, sent by the Trinity enthroned in Heaven, holds the Greek synonym *«ΟΜΟΟΥΣΙΟΣ»* (Consubstantial). On the right side of the painting a bishop in the vestments of the Eastern Church, with crown

99

and omophorion, the equivalent of the Roman pallium, is seated on a throne. He is apparently the imperial bishop Eusebius of Nicomedia, who played the role of mediator as a follower of Arius, then subscribed to the Nicene Creed, and later rejected it. Arianism survived its condemnation as late as the 7th century and was maintained by the Lombards, among others, as a type of national belief.

On a pedestal slightly to the right of the centre, on which there stands a deacon, the artist has placed his signature: «Jos. Wanenmacher Accad. Rom. invenit & pinxit 1762» (JOSEF WANNENMACHER, trained at the Roman Academy, conceived and painted these pictures, 1762).

(56) *The first Council of Constantinople in the year 381*
VISUM EST SPIRITU SANCTO ET NOBIS Act. 15. V. 28 (For it has pleased the Holy Ghost and us). The text, from the Acts of the Apostles, refers to the controversy concerning the mission to the heathen, which led to an apostolic council. The first Council of Constantinople was called by Emperor Theodosius I (reigned 379–395) for the purpose of settling differences of opinion and heresies concerning the divine person of the Holy Ghost. The Council took place in the Church of Anastasia in Constantinople, which is shown in Baroque splendour with a semi-circular choir. In the centre stands a Rococo altar, with two figures of martyrs with swords; in the tabernacle, a chalice with the Host. The clouds open into a light-flooded circle in which the Trinity is depicted. At the outer left side of the painting, on a canopied throne, sits Bishop Gregory of Nazianzus (ca. 330–390). Before him stands the Patriarch of Constantinople, Meletius of Antioch, who apparently died during the Council, and his student and follower, Flabius. Gregory was an important supporter of the concept of the divinity of the Holy Ghost, which the painter shows by the ray

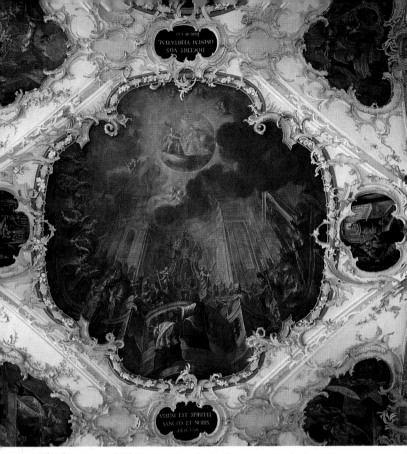

56 *The first Council of Constantinople. Ceiling painting in the Library, 1762, by Josef Wannenmacher.*

of light sent by the dove of the Holy Ghost which touches him. The bishop points to the text of the Creed, which hangs over the balustrade in the foreground: «ET IN SPIRITUM SANCTUM DOMINUM ET VIVIFI-CANTEM QUI EX PATRE FILIOQUE PROCEDIT» (I believe in the Holy Ghost, the Lord and giver of life, who proceeds from the Father and the Son). The ecclesiastics on the right are probably followers of the Macedonians or of the doctrine of Pneumatology, who denied the di-

101

vinity of the Holy Ghost. They were in the minority at this Council. The two acolytes on the steps in the foreground seem to be pointing to the Creed during the celebration of the mass. An oil sketch for this painting is in the Museum of Friedrichshafen.

⑤⑦ *The Council of Ephesus in the year 431*
At the top of the painting is the inscription «DOCEBIT VOS OMNEM VERITATEM. John 16 V. 13» (He [the Spirit of Truth] will teach you the whole truth). The verse is taken from the prophecies of the Lord on the action of the Holy Ghost after his death. The Council of Ephesus is a ratification of the doctrine expounded at Nicaea. The Council was called by the Emperor Theodosius II (reigned 408–450) during the pontificate of Coelestin I (reigned 422–432) and took place from 22 June to 17 July 431. Because Christ is identical in nature with the Son of God, the mother of Christ must be the mother of God (dogma of the Incarnation). The assembly place is shown as a Baroque background with columns. The altar picture shows Mary, described as «*ΘΕΟΤΟΚΟΣ*» (Mother of God); below her is a canopy with the inscription «AVE MARIA MATER DEI». The book lying on a throne bears a scarcely legible text: «ET VERBUM CARO FACTUM EST. Joh. 1,14» (And the Word was made flesh). To the right of the picture the patriarch Cyril of Alexandria sits under a canopy and defends the concept of the Mother of God against the Nestorians, who deny the motherhood of the Holy Virgin. The two letters spread out before him (Hebrew [?] writing not legible) probably refer to the correspondence between Cyril and Nestor, a priest of Constantinople.

The bishops arguing in groups are particularly striking. Above the scenery, Mary receives the glad tidings from the angel and the dove of the Holy Ghost descends towards her. The circle of stars refers to the woman of the Apocalypse, who was later identified with Mary. At

57 The Council of Ephesus. Ceiling painting in the Library, 1762, by Josef Wannenmacher.

the very top we see God the Father with the terrestrial globe, and on the left, suggesting the presence of Christ, the cross on an empty throne – a very unusual representation of the Trinity.

The Council of Chalcedon in the year 451   ⓢ⁸

In the cartouche at the top of the painting: «ECCE EGO VOBISCUM SUM. Matth. 28.V.20». The Gospel according to St.Matthew ends with these words of Christ: «Lo, I

103

am with you always, even unto the end of the world.» This Council, which had 600 participants, took place from 8 October to 1 November 451 and was convoked by the Emperor Markianos (reigned 450–457) during the pontificate of Pope Leo I (reigned 440–461), when the differences between Alexandria and Antioch concerning adherence to Nestorianism intensified. This fourth council promulgated the dogma of the two natures of Christ, the divine and the human. A synthesis between East and West was aimed at; but with this council began the theological alienation of the Eastern Church from Rome. The artist has placed the convocation of bishops in a central space with powerful archways, in which it is easy to recognize ressemblances to the just completed rotunda of the abbey church. In the centre is an altar, in front of which lies the figure of a young woman with a palm branch. She is identified as St.Euphemia, in whose church the Council took place. The scroll refers to the incarnation of Christ: «NATUS EX MARIA VIRGINE ET HOMO FACTUS EST» (He was born of the Virgin Mary and was made man). The text is reverently accepted by one bishop, and furiously rejected by another. These may be the patriarch Poterios (d. 457), who was inaugurated at Chelcedon, and the simultaneously deposed Dioskur (d. 454), who, together with Eutyches (d. 454) remained faithful to the doctrine of the single nature of Christ (Monophysitism). Even today this theological view continues to be held by the Copts. The applauding and the rejecting bishops are distributed on the right and left sides respectively. Above the scenery we again see the Trinity, with Christ indicated by a cross. In front of the Trinity the birth of Jesus is depicted.

The Doctors of the Church in the lunettes
The Latin Doctors of the Church, on the *west side: St.Gregory the Great, (Pope Gregory I, reigned 590–604).* Thanks to his outstanding personality, the papacy attained a new status in the Western world. His pontificate

58 *The Council of Chalcedon. Ceiling painting in the Library, 1762, by Josef Wannenmacher.*

was overshadowed by the wars of the Lombards, however. The 35 books of his Job commentaries became the «Moralia» of the Middle Ages. He was a patron of the liturgy and plainsong (Gregorian chant). The sheet with writing refers to Pope Gregory, the composer of the antiphony to the Blessed Virgin Mary «Regina Coeli Laetare Alleluja» (Rejoice, thou Queen of Heaven).

St.Ambrose (333/34–397), Bishop of Milan. Oldest ⑤⁹ of the Western Doctors of the Church and opponent of

105

Arianism. His writings on dogma are concerned above all with the Eucharist and the divine motherhood of Mary. Physically he is recognizable by the unevenness of his eyes. The beehive on the lower lefthand side refers to a legendary occurrence in the childhood of St.Ambrose, in which bees settled on his face without stinging him, a proof of celestial honey in his later discourses and writings.

St.Augustine (354–430), Bishop of Hippo, later Bone and now Annaba in Algeria. Son of the Christian Monica, he was first Manichaean and Neo-Platonist, but was then converted and baptized by St.Ambrose in Milan in the year 387. The most important theologian and Doctor of the Church of early Christendom («Confessiones» and «De Civitate Dei»). The putto with a spoon, his attribute, refers to the Augustinian conclusion that man is no more capable of fathoming the ultimate secrets of God than of draining the ocean with a spoon.

St.Jerome (ca. 347 – ca. 420). Born in Stridon, in Dalmatia, he died in Bethlehem. The painting shows the saint with bare torso, reminding us that he lived as a hermit for two years in the desert. The attributes of a lion and skull below and on his writing table emphasize the desolate nature of his surroundings. Above his head sounds a celestial trumpet which communicates the divine truths to him. Jerome translated the Holy Scriptures into Latin. Of this so-called Vulgate the Library possesses more than 100 fragments dating from around the year 420, from Italy (Ms. 1395). As a result of numerous voyages to Egypt and Palestine, Jerome became the intermediary between Western and Eastern Christianity. As he was briefly the private secretary of Pope Damasus (reigned 366–384), he is sometimes also portrayed as a cardinal.

At the back: St.Anselm of Canterbury (1033/34–1109). A native of Aosta, he became abbot of the Benedictine monastery of Bec in Normandy. In the Middle

106

Ages he was the most important interpreter of St.Augustine. He attempted to prove the tenets of the faith intellectually and was the author of important theological writings on the subject of the immaculate conception of Mary, which is why St.Anselm is portrayed as contemplating the Immaculate Conception. He was canonized in 1494, and raised to a Doctor of the Church in 1720 by Pope Clement XI.

On the short northern side: the Church. The Catholic Church is personified by a youthful figure holding a chalice with the Host and the keys of St.Peter. A tiara and ferule, as well as the domed building of St.Peter's Cathedral, represent the papacy. Behind the figure, the empty cross of Christ; above, the dove of the Holy Ghost, right, putto with open Gospel.

The *Greek Fathers of the Church* on the *east side:* individual identification presents a problem. All four figures wear bishops' vestments with cross-strewn mandyas

59 St.Ambrosius. Cartouche by Josef Wannenmacher, 1762; stucco work by Johann Georg and Mathias Gigl.

(pluvial) and omophorion (pallium) and have a crown and paterissa (crosier). The order is probably as follows:

St.Gregory of Nazianzus (330–389/90), Patriarch of Constantinople. This Cappadocian Doctor of the Church was the first great supporter of Christian humanism. Together with Basil the Great, he represented Nicene orthodoxy in the Arianic dispute. In the year 381 he took part in the Council of Constantinople. He could not continue as patriarch and withdrew to his country estate, where he wrote the theological discourses, letters and poems on which his fame is founded. His scholarship is indicated by a bookshelf and a putto carrying a book.

St.Basil the Great (329–379), Metropolitan (bishop) of Cappadocia. Together with his friend Gregory of Nazianzus, he supported the Nicene Creed. He developed the doctrine of the Trinity as it was subsequently defined at the Council of Constantinople. His life was shaped by

60 St.Basil the Great, Greek Father of the Church, by Josef Wannenmacher, 1762.

asceticism and social welfare work. He is known as the founder of Eastern monasticism. Our painting shows him kneeling before a picture of the Virgin Mary.

St.Athanasius the Great (ca. 295–373), Bishop of Alexandria. He was a student of the hermit Antonius. As deacon he accompanied the Bishop of Alexandria to the Council of Nicaea and became his successor. His relentless fight against the followers of Arianism forced him repeatedly into exile, for instance in Trier and in Rome, where he wrote his famous letters defending himself against defamatory accusations. His theological and historical writings sketch out a lively picture of those agitated times. In the painting he sits facing us; a putto points to a boat, probably a reference to his dangerous voyages.

St.John Chrysostomus (344/54–407), Patriarch of Constantinople. He was an ascetic on the bishop's throne and the greatest preacher of the Greek Church. His condemnation of the extravagant lifestyle of the imperial court earned him disfavour and banishment. He died in Pontus in exile. His sermons on various chapters of the Holy Scriptures are famous, especially on the letters of St.Paul. Indeed, our artist has placed him in the company of the Princes of the Apostles.

At the back: St.Bede the Venerable (672/73–735), an ⑥₁ English monk at the monastery of Wearmouth. His inclusion among the Doctors of the Church was – as in the case of St.Anselm opposite – an homage to the Benedictine order. Bede is the author of an English history and of important theological writings and chronicles. He was not named «Doctor Ecclesiae» until 1899, by Pope Leo XIII. The saint, who is only rarely depicted, is portrayed as a scholar, with a compass and terrestrial globe. In his left hand he holds *a magic number square.*

The number series always totals 34, horizontally, vertically and diagonally, as well as the four corner squares. In Christian times this number was related to

4	14	15	1
9	7	6	12
5	11	10	8
16	2	3	13

the age of Christ (1+33). Bede introduced the Christian chronology and wrote, among other things, «De schematibus et tropis», of which a copy made during the High Middle Ages is preserved in the Library (Ms. 878). The number square also appears – although mirror-inverted – in Duerer's famous engraving «Melancolia», of 1514. It is thought to go back to the Greek philosopher and mathematician Pythagoras (ca. 570–497/96 B.C.).

The small cartouches on the pendentives
The reddish and blue-grey painted scenes (known as grisaille painting) represent various disciplines of Benedictine scholarship which were to be found in the abbey library. The sequence alternates in accordance with the alphabetical library classifications in the gallery:

EE. Controversy theology. An old monk in an armchair points with his right hand to a text in a tome which a secular priest or preacher (?) holds on his knee. In the foreground, a table and draperies; at the back, bookcases.

FF. Asceticism. The abbot stands between two monks; the one on the left holds the Rule of St.Benedict «Reg(ula) S(ancti) P(atris) Bene(dicti)». From a small table on the right hangs a bookmark: «Ascet(ica) collat(iones) PP(atrum)».

II. Liturgy. Two monks take books from the shelves, the back of two of which are marked «Lyt(ani)ai, Lyt(urgiae)». At a table sits a third monk, writing. A bookmark hanging down bears the inscription «Sequentiae». On the right in the painting are a lectern and a column pedestal.

⑥② *KK. Theology.* In an ecclesiastical setting a monk stands in a round pulpit and reads from a book. Four novices listen and take notes. On the wall of books to the

61 St.Beda Venerabilis with magic number square, in the south east corner, by Josef Wannenmacher, 1762.

right we see theological works: «SS.PP. (Church Fathers), Theol(ogiae), Quaest(iones)».

NN. Geography. In a circular building with columns and books, which gives an impression of worldliness, with columns and books, two monks sit at a table and point to a map. Between them stands a globe, above which the monk on the left holds a compass. Left in the foreground, a globe and astronomical instruments.

OO. Medicine. Two individuals hold a discussion about a book in a pharmacy where, on the right, philosophical, medical and historical works are displayed: «Philo(sophia), Medic(ina), Gal(enos) (the last great phy-

111

sician of Antiquity), Hippoc(rates) (the famous physician of ancient times) and Arist(oteles). Left, on the shelves, receptacles and vials. In the foreground, a mortar and pestle.

RR. Historiography. Four monks sit in a book-filled cell at a round table, on which lie two books, marked «Chron(ologia)» and «vitae SS(anctorum)». The monk on the right holds a book entitled «Annales».

SS. Rhetoric. Three monks discuss a text in a work entitled «Orat(iones) Elegi(ae)». In the background, a wall of books and two windows; on the right, a column with drapery.

Above the entrance to the Manuscript Room, between TT and UU: *Bible commentary.* In a library, on the right-hand side at a long table, stands the master; two groups of three students each have taken their places at

62 Representation of Theology. Cartouche in a western pendentive, by Josef Wannenmacher, 1762.

the table. The first student on the left has a Greek book from which falls a sheet with the inscription «Graece gnosti, Act. 21», which refers to the point in the Acts of the Apostles where St.Paul, imprisoned in Jerusalem, is asked by the chief official: «Canst thou speak Greek?». The third monk from the left drops a paper with the words «Hebrei sunt et ego, 2. Cor. 11,22». Paul not only declared in front of the Jewish community that he himself was Jewish (Acts 22,3), but also wrote this in his second Letter to the Corinthians, to silence his opponents in the Jewish camp. A third writer shows the text «Haec scribimus vobis, 1. Joan 1,4». The apostle John wrote to his community: «Truly our fellowship is with the Father, and with his Son Jesus Christ. And these things write we unto you that your joy may be full.» A further reference is made to research in the abbey library and manuscript room in a cartouche at the top right-hand side «SCRU-TAMINI SCRIPTURAS, Joan 5,39» (Search the Scriptures).

Manuscript Room (no access)

The room where the manuscripts are kept is situated on the upper floor of the short southern side of the Library and is reached by the spiral staircase. The entrance has moulded and veneered wooden door jambs with Rococo intarsia; left, a youthful head with cap; right, a bearded head with a conical hat, accompanied in both cases by spiral- and foliage tendrils. Behind the iron door, of later date, is a small, rhomboid-shaped room with a tunnel-vault ceiling with three pairs of lunettes. Light enters through two elliptical-arched windows on the west and three round-arched windows on the south. *Rococo plaster mouldings* with rocailles, architectural motifs and small bunches of flowers in the style of the GIGL Brothers decorate the vault pendentives, the vertex and the window niches. The greenish background shade, the pink-coloured surfaces and the white plaster mouldings highlighted in gold make it possible – as in the Library – to guess the original colours, even though they have been painted over a number of times. The wood floor consists of walnut lozenges with fir panels. To the left and right of the entrance, and on the windowless east side, the room has matching furniture with beveled edges. Between the windows are free-standing cabinets with double doors; in the window niches low containers have been built in, the middle niche on the south side having been designed as a desk. The individual book cabinets bear small decorative plates with the serial number of the manuscripts, from 1 to 1506 and «subsequent». The western, «numophylacium» cabinet contains an important coin collection. In the centre of the room stand two more recent wooden items, one an 18th century carved lectern.

63 *Manuscript Room: book cupboards with intarsia decorations. Stucco work by the Gigl Brothers.*

All the cabinets along the walls are decorated with variously-stained walnut inlays within a mirror-image herring-bone frame, *figures in intarsia* and vertical moulding with flowing arabesques carved in relief. The set of nine matching cabinets have two pairs of pictures on each door in the rectangular fillets, making a total of 72. The bevel-edged cupboards, single cabinets and window ledges are decorated with 46 medallions of heads.

The themes – typical for that time, at the beginning of the period of Classicism – are taken from the world of the gods of antiquity. Illustrated books, which are still kept in the Library, were used as models: *Jacobus Gronovius, «Thesaurus Graecarum Antiquitatum», 10 volumes, Leyden 1697–1702.* The first volume, without numbered pages, was the inspiration for figure groups 11, 12, 17, 18 and 41. The seventh volume (foldout p.261) provided the models for most of the medallions: 1, 4, 7, 9–11, 13, 14, 17, 18, 21, 24, 25–29, 30, 33, 34–37, 39, 40–44.

However, the most important source was the *Handbook of Antiquity by Bernard de Montfaucon, revised by Johann Jakob Schatz, Antiquitates graecae et romanae, Nuernberg 1757 (Johann Salomon Semler).* The work, arranged like a dictionary, with a great number of engravings, was first published in London in 1721/22. It was acquired in 1758 during the time of the erudite abbey librarian Father Pius Kolb (1712–1762). The illustrations portray not only the world of the gods, but also the culture of the ancient world and moreover provide background information on the models on which they are based, the originals of which still have to be traced. The identification of the intarsia is based on the Latin legends contained in this book, although there is a danger that at that stage errors had already crept in. Only for the following scenes and medallions has it been impossible to discover the original models: 25, 42, 52, 67 and *5, 6, 19, 20.* These are exact individual mirror-image copies, enlarged three to four times, depending on the model.

64 *Manuscript Room: book cupboard, inlaid medallions depicting gods, about 1770.*

The strong outlines of the intarsia work have been burnt in, the incised parallel- and cross-hatchings coloured in with soot. The intarsia artist obviously attempted to give his work the appearance of an engraving. The choice of subject is entirely arbitrary and no attempt is made to

116

follow any particular plan. Gods and mythological scenes appear on the north wall, goddesses and muses on the short eastern front. The medallions too are only partly arranged by subject.

Brother GABRIEL LOSER (1701–1785), a monk of St.Gall, has long been considered not only to have made the furnishings for the Library, but also the furniture for the Manuscript Room. The famous «Arcularius» (jewelry box maker), he reveals himself here as an outstanding artist and craftsman. He headed an efficient monastery workshop where, among others, Brother THADDAEUS KUSTER (1731–1800) of Eschenbach in the Canton of St.Gall, and Brother PAUL WUECHERER (1736–1800) of Karsee (District of Ravensburg) also worked. A skilled draughtsman, Brother GABRIEL probably prepared the designs, which must then have been transferred to the wood by a number of hands. Close examination reveals marked artistic differences in the execution of the faces and limbs, which appear crude and coarse in comparison with the model drawings.

The intarsia in the Manuscript Room constitute one of the most *extensive examples of this type of art* in Switzerland; in terms of theme, also, they have scarcely any equals for comparison. They must have been produced in the late 1760s and in the 1770s.

The intarsia with mythological subjects in the Manuscript Room
(see diagram p.118)

Figures: 1. Venus and Adonis. – 2. Venus Marina. – 3. The seven days on the boat. – 4. Medusa. – 5. Pan and Apollo. – 6. Sun and moon. – 7. Oceanus. – 8. Pluto and Cerberus. – 9. Ajax and Cassandra with a statue of Minerva. – 10. Hercules with the columns of Atlas. – 11. Ganymede with the eagle of Zeus. – 12. Bellarophon tames Pegasus. – 13. Bellonarius with Bellona. – 14. Saturn with bound feet, bowed over a scythe. – 15. Leda and Zeus in the form of an eagle. – 16. Minerva and Venus. – 17. Europa abducted by Zeus in the form of a bull. – 18. The Fates Lachesis and Atropos. – 19. Eros and Anteros. – 20. Silvanus in the form of Pan before a herm. – 21. Cybele on lions. – 22. Three women with offerings. – 23. Jupiter between Hygeia and As-

117

clepius. – 24. Juno and Vesta. – 25. A god waving a feather in front of a column (unidentified). – 26. Vulcan. – 27. Venus Caelestis. – 28. Cupid crucifies Psyche in the form of a butterfly. – 29. Hermes kills the cyclops Argus. – 30. Vesta with a statue of Roma. – 31. Saturn with torch. – 32. Actaeon transformed into a deer by Diana. – 33. Hippomenes

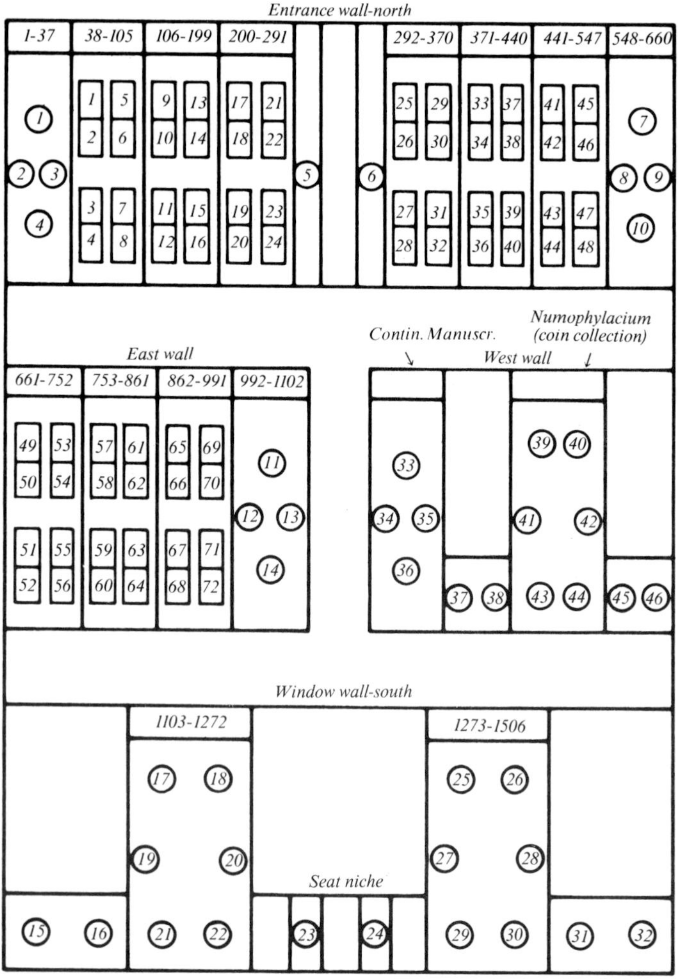

Entrance wall-north

| 1-37 | 38-105 | 106-199 | 200-291 | | | 292-370 | 371-440 | 441-547 | 548-660 |

Contin. Manuscr.

Numophylacium (coin collection)

East wall

West wall

| 661-752 | 753-861 | 862-991 | 992-1102 |

Window wall-south

| 1103-1272 | | 1273-1506 |

Seat niche

and Atalanta. – 34. Hercules tames Cerberus. – 35. Dedalus shapes a wing. – 36. The so-called «Jupiter of Brixen». – 37. Hercules vanquishes Antaeus. – 38. Zeus hurling lightning. – 39. Mercury. – 40. Aesculapius. – 41. Alpheus unites with the source Arethusa. – 42. Seated woman with shield and scroll (unidentified). – 43. Hecate triplex. – 44. Zeus-Ammon in the form of a bird (oracle). – 45. Neptune with two seahorses. – 46. Hygeia with serpents. – 47. Four-faced Janus with bow. – 48. Saturn with terrestrial globe. – 49. The Muse Clio (history). – 50. The muse Calliope (epic poetry). – 51. The Flower. – 52. Goddess with half-moon, statuette of Nike and rooster, probably Athena. – 53. The muse Euterpe (music). – 54. The muse Urania (astronomy). – 55. Bacchus with Ariadne. – 56. The goddess Juno with a child (as helper at births. – 57. The muse Melpomene (tragedy). – 58. The muse Thalia (comedy). – 59. Pomona with fruit. – 60. The goddess Diana. – 61. The muse Terpsichore (dance). – 62. Vesta Tuccia as a water carrier. – 63. Ceres on the terrestrial globe. – 64. Minerva in armour. – 65. The muse Erato (lovesong). – 66. Hope. – 67. Woman with a veil and torch (unidentified). – 68. Vestal virgin with sacrificial fire. – 69. The muse Polyhymnia (classical song). – 70. The goddess Isis. – 71. Diana Lucifer. – 72. Minerva with lance and shield.

The medallions: 1 Mercury – 2 Medusa – 3 Isis and Serapis – 4 Isis – 5 Head in profile, with laurel wreath (unidentified) – 6 King in profile (unidentified) – 7 Pax – 8 Cybele – 9 Pallas Athene – 10 Hercules – 11 Cupid – 12 Woman with circlet of fruit (unidentified) – 13 Hygeia – 14 Pietas – 15 Sphynx – 16 Osiris – 17 Salus – 18 Clementia – 19 Female head in profile (unidentified) – 20 Female head in profile (unidentified) – 21 Fides – 22 Justitia – 23 Sol and Luna – 24 Castor and Pollux – 25 Janus – 26 Juno sospita – 27 Neptune – 28 Diana – 29 Sarapis – 30 Mars – 31 Female head in profile on moon (Diana?) – 32 Aesculapius – 33 Felicitas – 34 Cybele – 35 Bacchus – 36 Jupiter Anxyr. – 37 Bacchus – 38 Medusa – 39 Vulcan – 40 Ceres – 41 Canopus – 42 Saturn – 43 Jupiter-Ammon – 44 Pluto – 45 Fauna – 46 Faunus.

The Manuscript Collection

The Library, which comprises approximately 130,000 volumes, possesses more than 1650 incunabula and early imprints and about 2000 manuscripts, the majority of which originated in the St.Gall scriptorium. The art of the miniature in St.Gall attained a peak during the time of Abbot Grimalt (ruled 841–872), Abbot Hartmut (ruled 872–883) and Abbot-Bishop Salomon (ruled 890–

⑥⑥ 919). During that period were produced the *Folchart Psalter* (Ms. 23) with its superb gold initial letters and the *Golden Psalter* (Ms. 22) with its many figures illustrating the story of King David. The *ivory book covers* are particularly precious. According to the most recent research, the narrow, decoratively carved tablets of *Codex 60* were made for Charlemagne himself in about 800 and were used by him as writing tablets. In an imitation of this courtly art, the monk TUOTILO carved two ivory tablets of equal artistic calibre for the *Evangelium Longum* (Ms. 53), representing the Assumption of the Blessed Virgin Mary, and the legend of St.Gallus and the bear. The Late Classical ivory covers of *Codex 359* with mythological scenes portraying the combat of the gods with the Indians are a curiosity; they were carved in about the year 500 in Ostrom. Apart from the manuscripts produced in St.Gall, there are also *108 pre-Carolingian manuscripts* of other origins, including the oldest manuscript of the Vulgate Bible, dating from about the year 420 (Ms. 1395), fragments of Virgil from the 5th century (Ms. 1394), and *15 Irish manuscripts* of the 7th to 12th centuries, including a Latin manuscript of the Gospels (Ms. 51) with 12 full-page miniatures, dating from about the year 750, which have a unique place in the history of book illumination in the Early Middle Ages because of the abstract quality of their calligraphy and ornamentation.

The *plan of the monastery of St.Gall* is of world renown; it was brought to St.Gall by two monks from Reichenau in about the year 820, approximately ten years before the beginning of construction under Abbot Gozbert (ruled 816–837). This unique parchment document is a plan for an ideal monastic community of the Early Middle Ages, only the beginnings of which were to be achieved, however, at St.Gall.

During the High Middle Ages St.Gall lost its artistic pre-eminence to other monasteries. A *book cover from*

Limoges with opaque enamel work depicting the crucifixion and Christ in Majesty (Ms. 216) dates from about the year 1200. Among the *manuscripts of the Late Middle Ages* must be mentioned a few particularly richly illuminated examples: Codex 602, with 140 illustrations of the life of St.Gallus and other saints, dated 1460; Codex 643, with 80 pen and ink drawings illustrating the fables of Ulrich Bonner; and, above all, the book of armoury of

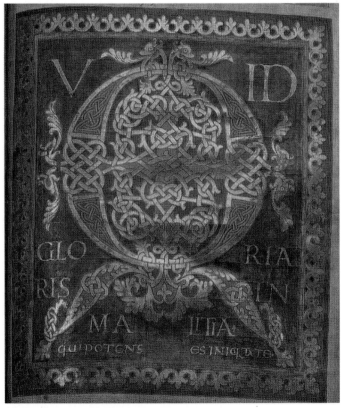

66 Carolingian gold initial Q in the Folchart Psalter, made between 864 and 872.

121

HANS HAGGENBERG (Ms. 1084), of importance to heraldry, with the personal inscription of the Winterthur artist, 1488.

During the *Renaissance,* St.Gall again achieved eminence in Switzerland in the art of miniature painting and manuscript writing. Thanks to their signatures, two artists, NIKLAUS BERTSCHI of Rorschach and CASPAR HAERTLI of Lindau, are known to us; the former a master of ornamental initials and borders (Mss. 534 and 535, ca. 1517/20); the latter standing out for his large-format pages of pictures and the decorative arms of the contemporary abbots of the monastery (Mss. 541 and 542, dated 1544 and 1562).

The Lapidarium

In the Baroque cellar of the west wing, which can be reached through the porch of the Cathedral or through the western side of the cloister-walk, there is an important collection of architectural sculpture of the Middle Ages. As far as is known, no pre-Baroque construction survives within the monastery precinct. Our knowledge of the lay-out of the monastery during the Middle Ages is based on the one hand on pictorial documents which have been preserved, and, on the other, on evidence from excavations and on relatively few, but highly important, architectural remains.

The rough stonework of the groined vault and the inserted pillars, the eastern row of which corresponds to the cloister-walk above it, were whitewashed for the presentation of the exhibits in 1981. The niches are eminently suitable for displaying the stone evidence of the architectural history of the monastery. In the recesses are Carolingian and Ottonian items from the 9th and 10th centuries; in the south corner finds from the 15th to 17th centuries. The presentation was the idea of Hans Rudolf Sennhauser, who, with Benedikt Frei, headed the excavations in the Cathedral.

67 Lapidarium in the Baroque cellar of the west wing. Carolingian, Ottonian and Late Gothic finds.

To the east of the entrance stairs are informative *plans*. On the table, a facsimile of the Carolingian monastery plan of around 820, from Reichenau (original in the Library), shows an almost square architectural arrangement with enclosed church, cloister and surrounding workshops and agricultural buildings – the ideal monastic community of the Early Middle Ages. Since the excavations in the 1960s we know that the abbey church built by Abbot Gozbert in about 830 deviated from this plan. Nevertheless, it can be assumed that it was only in the Late Middle Ages that the compact architectural arrangement was broken up to take the form recorded by the St.Gall monk Father GABRIEL HECHT (1664–1745) in his very precise and informative ground plan of 1719. The heterogeneous complex, surrounded from 1566 by the so-called partition wall, consisted of scattered individual buildings. Only the church and the cloister indi-

123

cate the core dating from the Early- and High Middle Ages. At that time the Carolingian nave of the Gallus church, the Late Gothic chancel and tower still existed, as did the Early Baroque Otmar church to the west. The Late Gothic cloister and the western library wing of 1551/53 were then also still extant. However, only the eastern section of the monastery and the palace wing (abbey), both dating from the late 17th century, have survived until the present time.

The excavation plan of the abbey church shows, within the Late Baroque walls, the foundations (marked in red) of the Carolingian church built between approximately 830 and 837. This church had three naves and corresponded in length to the present-day chancel and rotunda. The walls running parallel on each side of the chancel delimited a subterranean walk, which opened into the east crypt. The tomb of St.Gallus lay in the monks' chancel in front of the steps of the present-day high altar. Not much later, an intermediate building arose to the west of the Gallus church, the so-called «Helmhaus», onto which the Otmar church was built in 867 and, in about 980, the still extant Otmar crypt.

After the devastating fire of 1418 in the abbey church, Prince-Abbot Ulrich Roesch (ruled 1463–1491) first of all built the Gothic triple-nave chancel, the foundation walls of which have been drawn in yellow on a detailed plan. The red dots indicate the Carolingian components, which at that time formed part of the pillar foundations. They were discovered during the most recent excavations, removed, and in 1981 exhibited here. Two photographs show the position of the finds in 1964/65.

Early Medieval components
The five capitals, the four imposts and the remains of bases, all of Rorschach sandstone, belong to the Gozbert church of about 830 and indicate an imposing basilica

with columns. The variously sculpted *capitals and imposts are among the most brilliant and greatest testimony to Carolingian architectural sculpture.* The forms range from low reliefs of the Carolingian guilloche type to Classical Corinthian foliage.

Nos. 1, 9, 16. The rectangular impost blocks have reliefs of standing reeds, which are connected by a rod at the bottom of the outstretched leaf tips and are crowned with a rope.

No. 2. A substantial capital with hanging ornaments made by the chip-carving technique, leaves with palmettes under volute arches. There is a noticeable stylistic resemblance to the Carolingian marble plaque from Lauterach in the Landesmuseum in Bregenz.

Nos. 3, 5. Both capitals have a necking with cable moulding, surmounted by arches with small tongues. Fan-like leaves grow from the upper part, rolling up in a snail-shape at the corners (broken off in no. 3). The front of no. 5 has birds (heavily damaged) picking at a grape, with a vine leaf above. The ornamentation is reminiscent of the Carolingian capital and the lattice-work plaques from the church of Schaenis, which were made in about 820 (now in a protected room in Schaenis).

Nos. 7, 8. The two capitals, similar in their curling ornaments, have stylized acanthus motifs with overlapping heracleum leaves and arched frames on twisted supports. This is the most stylistically developed piece in the collection.

Nos. 4, 6, 20. The first two imposts are comparable with capital no. 2 with regard to the palmette ornamentation. The encircling «croix patté» crosses are a new element in no. 4. In no. 20, below the palmette fans, two birds pick at a grape.

Nos. 10–22. The fragments of column bases, shaped bottom pieces and simpler capitals yield, for the careful observer interested in architectural history, information on the structure, building technique and size of the Ca-

125

rolingian church. The richly stepped bases of nos. 10–12 must have supported great columns, the base rings of which have a greater diameter than those of the capitals, which indicates that the probably very high shafts tapered towards the top. Pillar base no. 14 belonged to the Carolingian parclose and was found in the church in situ.

No. 23–25. The three Ottonian, un-restored cushion capitals from the Otmar crypt date from about the year 980. They have been replaced by copies at their original site.

Nos. 26–29. Dressed stone finds from the east and west crypts.

Late- and Post-Gothic finds
The objects come from the Late Gothic choir *(nos. 30–33),* the rood screen *(nos. 37–42)* and the cloister walk *(nos. 43–46)* as well as from the library building of 1551/53 and from buildings that have not been precisely identified. Many pieces bear traces of colour from the

68 *Carolingian capital from the church of Abbot Gozbert, about 830, found in 1964.*

original (?) polychromatic decoration. The fragments of a female figure *(no. 47)* and of a male head *(no. 48)* reveal, despite damage, excellent artistic quality. Of four much damaged keystones with busts *(no. 49)*, only one monk can be made out, on the right (St.Otmar?) (mid-16th century).

No. 50. Three keystones with well-preserved half-figures of St.Jerome with lions, St.Wiborada with a (broken) halberd and St.Scholastica with a book and dove, all with partially legible scrolls (ca. 1520/30). They were found in the substructure of a pilaster of the Otmar church of 1623. ⑦

No. 51. Twelve polychrome keystones from the library building of Abbot Diethelm Blarer, 1551. The foundation for this magnificent building, which apparently was a double-naved, two-storeyed, ribvaulted hall, was ceremonially laid on 6 July 1551 in the presence of ecclesiastical and lay dignitaries, and of the entire monastery (see Library Ms. 1253). Construction was completed in 1553. The keystones displayed the arms of members of the chapter at St.Gall. They were found in 1954 in the south wing of the cloister. From left to right:

Above. 1. Imperial arms with double eagle. 2. Left: Arms showing a pruning-knife between two vines on three peaks, initials destroyed, belonging to Br. Heinrich Sailer of Wil (professed 1509, d. 1560), founder and briefly (1546) abbot of St.Johann in the Thurtal. Right: Arms destroyed, initials ??B. 3. Arms of Abbot Diethelm Blarer (ruled 1530–1564) with the bear of the monastery of St.Gall and the mastiff of the county of Toggenburg. 4. Left: Arms with a climbing bear in front of a flowering branch, initials destroyed, belonging to Dean Jakob Bertz of Roggwil (d. 1552). Right: Arms with a red dragon, belong to Br. Johann Georg Mangolt of Constance (professed 1538, d. 1567). 5. Escutcheon with monogram ⚜ (unidentified) and arms with a vine. Of the initials, only the final W has been preserved. These may be the emblem and arms of the master builder. 6. Left: Arms with a leaping ibex and the initials F.B.S., belonging to Br. Balthasar Schmid of Diessenhofen (professed 1548, d. 1575). Right: head of a bird with a clover leaf in its beak and the initials F.I.R., belonging to Br. Johann Rhyner of Ueberlingen (professed 1548, d. 1571). 7. Stone with the inscription «DIETHELMUS. DEI. ET. APPOSTOLIC(E). SEDIS. GRACIA. ABBAS. MONAS-TERY. SANTI. GALLI. ANNO. MILLESIM(O). QVIN-GENTESIM(O. QV)INQVAGESIMO. VNO». (Diethelm, by the grace of God and the Apostolic Seat, Abbot of the Monastery of St.Gall, in the year 1551). 8. Left: Arms with two hens and the initials F.I.H., belonging to Br. (H)ieronimus Henner of Ueberlingen (professed 1545, d. 1557). Right: Rose branch with the initials F.M.B., belonging to Br. Martin Bickhard of Reichenau (professed 1538, d. 1555). 9. Left: Oak leaves with an acorn and the initials F.H.L., belonging to Br. Hans Landsberger of Rapperswil (professed 1548, d.? in Rheinau), perhaps a brother of Heinrich Landsberger, abbot of Fischingen (ruled 1556–1565); right, two animal traps (?) and a crown with the initials H??, perhaps belonging to Br. Maurus Harsch (professed 1538, d. 1574). 10. Left: damaged arms with standing cotyledon and the initials F.S.?, belonging to Br. Heinrich Keller of Rapperswil (1518–1567), sub-prior and an important composer and calligrapher; right, arms with crossed swords, initials destroyed, not identified. 11. Left: Wild man, initials destroyed, belonging to Br. Joachim Waldmann of Wangen (Bavaria) (professed 1538, d. 1551). Waldmann's arms also appear at the «Court» in Wil, where he was Governor. Right: Inscription destroyed and arms damaged: two crescent moons, turned away from each other, cover a pestle placed crosswise, belonging to Br. Jakob Stoessel of Rapperswil (professed 1533, d. 1582), priest in Wil in 1551. 12. Left: Heavily damaged arms with a snake and the initials F.O.K., belonging to Br. Otmar Kunz of Wil (professed 1547, d. 1577), later abbot. Right: Arms destroyed, initials F.C.W., belonging to Br. Christoph Wolber of Ravensburg (professed 1547, d. 1556).

No. 52. Four keystones with arms: above, Abbot Diethelm Blarer with the arms of the monastery; in the centre, Otmar Kunz twice; below heavily damaged arms with globes (?), possibly the arms of Pope Pius IV Medici (reigned 1559–1565) (see the Charles Borromeo Gate, p.197.)

No. 53. Two ribs and a Renaissance console from the library building of about 1551.

No. 54. Shell fragment, about 1551.

69 *Boss from the old Library, 1551; arms of F. Balthazar Schmid and F. Johann Rhyner.*

70 *Late Gothic boss with relief of the Church Father Jerome, about 1520/30. Original site unknown.*

No. 55. Baptismal font of Alpine limestone, 17th century, origin unknown.

No. 56. Mantelpiece with the arms of Abbot Otmar Kunz (ruled 1564–1577) in palmette.

Nos. 57–59. Ribs and rib imposts, probably from the Late Gothic cloister. On the surfaces, Roman numbers.

The South Wing

The west and south wings were rebuilt simultaneously in 1758/59 under the direction of PETER THUMB and his

130

son. The buildings form a powerful angle and now present a uniform external appearance with four full storeys, single windows and a mansard hipped roof, the two wings having the angle projection in common. The south wing has a distinctive central projection. The new central portal has a double door with a relief sculpture of a monk and is surmounted by two sandstone reliefs of three teaching monks and three students by AUGUST RAUSCH, 1955. Behind this, accessible from the cloister, is the impressive *staircase,* the shaft of which, surrounded by pillars, goes up to a landing on pillars. The staircase is bordered by balusters of red marble up to the second floor, and further up by marble-veneered wood. The uniformly vaulted ground floor rooms were the refectory, workshops and service areas; they can no longer be identified precisely. The wing is at present used by the Catholic Cantonal School, which also uses the ground floors in the west and east wings. The vaulted cellar below the south wing corresponds to that in the west wing (Lapidarium). Part of it has been arranged as a storage room for valuable objects from the Library.

⑦

The East Wing

The High Baroque section was built in 1674 by DANIEL GLATTBURGER during the time of Abbot Gallus Alt. It consisted of the chapter hall (where the Chapel of the Sacred Heart now stands (see p.134), the kitchen, and on the two upper floors, the monks' cells. A large cellar with a tunnel vault was built in the basement, and is used today as an auditorium for theatre and film presentations of the school. At the same time (or earlier?) the well still in existence was dug in the north cellar. In the course of the Late Baroque reconstruction of the monastery quarters, the east wing obtained, in 1763, under the direction of FERDINAND BEER, an additional storey with a saddleback roof, which was restored in 1957. At present the building is used mainly for the *administration of the diocese* and as the *residence of the dean* (previously the dean of the monastery), which is why it is also known as the

71 *Staircase in the south wing, to the Library. Built by Peter Thumb, 1758/59.*

Dean's Wing. The *archives of the diocese* are also kept here. In 1959, on the occasion of the 1,200th-anniversary feast-day of St.Otmar, the Catholic Administration had an *Otmar fountain* with reliefs and a standing figure of the Saint built in what is known as the Brunnenhof (fountain courtyard). This fountain is the work of AUGUST RAUSCH, and depicts Waltram presenting Otmar to King Pippin; Abbot Otmar receiving monks, helping the poor, being arrested and taken to prison in Bodman; and the body of Otmar being rowed across Lake Constance.

The strikingly bare edifice is flanked on the south by the *«Study House»*, which was probably built at the same time and is today the seat of the Catholic Administration, and by the *northern palace wing* of 1666, the present-day residence of the Bishop. In the south corner of the fountain courtyard, a ground-level passage leads to the former «Rekreirgarten» (recreation garden), the present school playground. On the east facade is a resplendent Baroque *sandstone coat of arms,* carved in 1674 by a ⑦⑥ sculptor named JOHANNES, showing the arms of the sponsor of the building, Abbot Gallus. On the roof top is a turret with an onion dome. The portal to the fountain courtyard has a *sculpted crowning scroll* with the inscription «RELIGIONI SCIENTIIS ET ARTIBUS PIE REDDITUM IN IPSO FESTO S.GALLI MDCCCIX» (Reverently returned to Religion, the Sciences and the Arts, on the feast of St.Gallus, 1809). The text refers to the founding of a Catholic secondary school in the abbey building, which had been abandoned in 1805; it continues to flourish today as the Catholic Cantonal School. The spacious vestibule with the stairway to the upper floors is of recent origin. Along the west wall stand two large recently restored *Early Baroque statues* of St.Gallus ⑦④ and St.Otmar. They probably originally adorned the high altar of the Otmar church and, accordingly, would be the work of the Constance sculptor HANS SCHENCK in about

133

1625. Along the south wall is a new *memorial tablet* made of sandstone, in which a zinc tablet, dated 1 May 1674, set into the foundation stone and discovered in 1957, bears the names of those involved in the construction: the artisan DANIEL GLATTBURGER, «Cementarius» (mason) of Rotmont, the carpenters GALLUS and JAKOB FALCK of Straubenzell and the stonecutter BALTHASAR ZERLAUT of Blumenegg (?), as well as the names of the chapter members of the time. Below that is a sandstone coat of arms of the monastery, with the bear, dating from the mid-16th century. The south door leads into the present *music room,* which is still occasionally called the «traiterie» in reference to the kitchen and refectory which were formerly located here. On the walls of the restored room hang *paintings of the nine last abbots of St.Gall.*

The Chapel of the Sacred Heart (Herz-Jesu-Kapelle)
To the north of the vestibule, accessible from the cloister, is the *Chapel of the Sacred Heart,* formerly known as «St.Mary in the Enclosure». The room was originally used as the chapter house and because of the lack of windows also bore the name «capella nigra» (dark chapel). On the modern door are two angel reliefs by AUGUST RAUSCH, 1957. The flat plaster ceiling of the nave, by MATHIAS GIGL, 1764/65, restored in 1957, has a representation of the eye of God in stucco work and the moulding has large, pale-green rocaille ornamentation and flower garlands. Behind the shallow choir arch is a rhomboid-shaped, obviously renovated room, which receives light through a window facing south onto the courtyard. The Baroque altar has been greatly changed and now bears the arms of Augustinus Egger, Bishop of St.Gall (reigned 1882–1906). The base is adorned by an exquisite *bronze relief* depicting the gathering of manna. It is part of a series of similar plaques on the side altars of the Cathedral, made by FRANZ ANTON DIRR in about

134

1770 (see p.43). The painting of the crucifixion is by AL-BERT SCHENKER, 1957. In the atrium of the chapel, which belongs to the cloister in spatial terms, is a tablet set up in the late 19th century, in the form of an epitaph, with the names of the church patrons and abbots of St.Gall up until 1805. We are reminded of the time of the monastery by a small bell kept in a partly glassed-in, marbled Baroque case along the northern separating wall. In those days it rang the hours five minutes early, as it still does, so that the monks would not be late for the chancel offices. A carved *Rococo door* leads to the northern side of the cloister.

The *staircase* of the above-mentioned entrance hall leads to the upper floors. Its Baroque character is seen principally in its perfectly shaped balusters and elegant handrail, by JOSEF SCHWAIGER, 1765/66. On the first floor we find ourselves in a spacious hall with central

72 Sacred Heart Chapel in the east wing. Vault stucco work by Mathias Gigl, 1764/65. Alteration of Baroque altar.

wooden pillars, the base of which still shows a Gothic pattern. The ceiling and joists have been plastered. The eastern doorway leads to the present-day bishop's residence (previously the abbey), and the northern door to the upper sacristy. Along the north wall a staircase leads directly into the south-east corner of the church, which gave the monks internal access to the chancel. The Baroque clock is connected with the striking mechanism referred to above.

(73) Along the *corridor,* which is wider than the cloister-walk below it, are the former cells of the monks, today the offices of the diocesan administration. The Baroque wooden *doors with columns* have been much restored

73 East wing, built 1674, altered 1763. Corridor on first floor, with former monks' cells.

and only the second door still has Rococo carvings. The second floor is similarly arranged and is at present lived in by the dean (no access). The upper (third) floor has further monastic cells with simple door-frames.

In the hall of the first and second floors there are *Baroque wooden statues* of Christ and the twelve apostles. These originally came from the parish church of St.Martin in Bruggen, which was demolished in 1936. An artist's inscription in St.Peter's book ascribes the figures, which are a little smaller than life-size, to the Ueberling sculptor FRANZ ANTON DIRR, 1784. Apart from the partially restored polychromatic decoration, the style seems to belong to a previous period and it is tempting to ascribe an earlier date to the work. Was DIRR only its (later?) painter or is the stiffness of Classicism already noticeable here?

On the front of the cell doors there are a total of *eight paintings on canvas* in grisaille: five perspective views of Swiss Benedictine monasteries with accompanying historical texts and three laudatory tablets with Latin maxims, which allow decoding of the difficult emblems. Originally there probably were nine pairs of pictures, corresponding to the number of Benedictine monasteries in Switzerland. A further perspective view of the monastery of St.Gall from this series is found in the Library.

The pictures were painted in about 1760, inspired by the «Idea», a jubilee publication printed in 1702 on the occasion of the centenary of the existence of the Swiss Benedictine congregation at St.Gall. At least some of the drawings for that publication had been provided by the St.Gall monk Father GABRIEL HECHT, and at least some of the engravings by JAKOB MULLER of Augsburg. In comparison with these, our tablets lack the portrait of the abbot of 1702, and the surrounding landscape has been freely interpreted.

1. The Monastery of Einsiedeln: MONASTERIUM PRINCIPALE EINSIDLENSE. At the side: Death of

74 *St.Gallus. Early Baroque wood statue, about 1625, in the east wing.*
75 *Allegorical tablet from the Monastery of Muri, about 1760, in the east wing.*

St.Meinrad and St.Eberhard (?). 2. The Monastery of Fischingen: MONASTERIUM FISCHINGENSE. At the side: St.Idda of Toggenburg and a deer hunt of the Count of Toggenburg. 3. The Monastery of Disentis: MONASTERIUM DISERTINENSE. At the side: St.Sigisbert and St.Placidus. 4. The Monastery of Engelberg: MONASTERIUM MONTIS ANGELORUM. At the side: Abbot Adelhelm and the death of the monastery founder Konrad von Seldenbueren. 5. The Monastery of Mariastein: MONASTERIUM B.V. IN PETRA. At the side. Abbot Esso and a church, probably the previous small monastery of Beinwil. 6. (In the Library) The Monastery of St.Gall: MONASTERIUM PRINCIPALE S.GALLI. At the side: St.Gallus, and St.Otmar's miracle of the wine at Lake Constance. 7. Eulogy of the Monastery of Einsiedeln. The painting shows large-scale perspectives of a park, described as Elysium in the text. The virgin in the grotto refers to Maria Einsiedeln, the angelic dance to the initiation of the angels. Title inscriptions: «CONGREGATIO EXORNAT» (To the credit of the [Benedictine] Congregation). «Maiorem unita decorum» (United, it is a greater ornament). Eulogy of the Monastery of ⑦ Muri. The painting shows an ideal city with twelve gates and walls adorned with jewels, a reference to the Latin word «muri» (walls). Title inscriptions: «CONGREGATIO NOBILITAT» (The [Benedictine] Congregation ennobles); «Pretium concordibus augent» ([The gems] increase the lustre of the order). Eulogy of the Monastery of Pfaefers. The painting shows a landscape with a brook (it differs from the original engraving, which shows the spa in the gorge of the Tamina). A dove swooping down refers to the founding legend of St.Pirmin. Title inscriptions: «CONGREGATIO ASSOCIAT» (The congregation joins together); «Compare gaudet» (We rejoice equally).

At the end of the corridor hangs a large *portrait* of the first bishop of the diocese of St.Gall, established in 1847, Johannes Mirer (reigned 1847–1862).

On the third floor there are *three further allegorical tablets* belonging to the «Idea» series, but they are difficult to interpret despite long Latin commentary texts in distichs. 1. «SCIENTIA – Facit esse Deus» (Science enables us to be like gods). In the cartouche, a landscape with the tree of knowledge, described in the text as the cedar of Sfondrati (Abbot Coelestin Sfondrati [ruled 1687–1696] was renowned as a great scholar). The serpent which encircles the tree trunk is the symbol of both wisdom and temptation. On the left, a man with torches stands in front of groups of listening people, on the right a rider falls from a rearing horse. The scenes refer to the duty of the monastery to disseminate knowledge, and also to the danger of presumption. 2. «DISCIPLINA – A rigore viror» (Discipline – Severity makes me strong). The cartouche shows a large tree among smaller trees (Paradise); in front, St.Michael with a sword. On the left,

139

Adam and Eve in the field; right, a man with a plough, probably a reference to mankind having to toil after the loss of Paradise. The text is half Greek, half Latin (with mistakes). 3. «BONITAS – Duplex Anagramma: Sat boni, at bonis» (Charity – Double play on words: many good things but only for the good ones). The picture shows another landscape of Paradise; beneath a great tree, domestic and wild animals are united in friendship. Left, a man with a book in front of the statue of a god (?), right, a landscape. The text is written in Hebrew on one half, and in Latin on the other (mistakes).

In the same corridor hang a further *two large engravings:* a text extolling the house of Habsburg and the reigning emperor, Charles VI, by GEORG PHILIPP RUGENDAS of Augsburg, 1727, and a bird's eye view of Rome, engraved for King Charles III of Spain, 1765.

76 Sculpted arms of Abbot Gallus Alt on the east facade of the east wing, about 1674.

The Palace Wing

(Now the residence of the Bishop and part of the administration buildings)

The building along the south side of the monastery square was given its present form during the time of Abbot Gallus Alt, in 1666/67. The plans were drawn up by two well-renowned Grison architects, GIOVANNI SERRO and GIULIO BARBIERI, both of Roveredo in Mesocco. The work was carried out by the master builder DANIEL GLATTBURGER, who was also to build the east wing of the monastery quarter in 1674 (see p.134). The residence of the abbot was situated in the western section. The eastern section comprised the palace and state administration, the kitchens, bakery and pharmacy, as well as the guest rooms and dining room. Between the two sections there opened an archway with the monastery gate. When FERDINAND BEER took on the construction of the new palace in 1767, he also lengthened the palace wing and sacrificed the two turrets in the eastern corner in favour of a corner connection, which provided access to the medieval round tower (see p.193). After the dissolution of the monastery in 1805, the palace wing became for a time the property of the newly-founded canton. On the establishment of the joint diocese of Chur and St.Gall in 1824, the Catholic Administration acquired the former abbot's residence and established the bishop's residence there. While the outside has remained largely unchanged since the time of the monastery, the inside underwent far-reaching alterations.

The three-storeyed palace wing, which has three rows of some 21 windows each, divides the fountain courtyard adjacent to the south from the monastery square proper. The strikingly austere construction, with a light rhythm imparted by the windows, has a saddleback roof with staggered dormer windows, interrupted

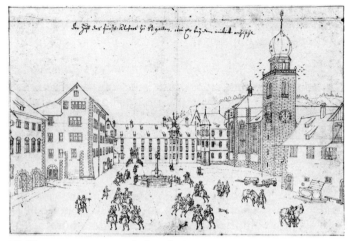

77 *The monastery square before the Late Baroque constructions. Drawing by Johann Melchior Fuessli, after 1709. Zentralbibliothek Zurich.*

by a gable which has been pushed through transversally above the stairwell. In the fourth section from the west there is a *polygonal turret* with an onion dome and a Christogram above the rain spout. In the ninth section is a *gateway.* At the top of its arch on the outer side are the emblems of the Canton (fasces) and of the bishopric of St.Gall (a mitre), in place of the former architectural sculpture with figures of St.Gallus and St.Otmar (said to be the ones which are now above the choir stalls in the Cathedral). A doorway further to the east leads via a steep staircase to the spacious tunnel-vaulted *cellar,* which stretches under the entire palace wing, with the exception of the eastern section. The ground-floor windows have diamond-shaped lattice-work screens. The rain-spout and the onion dome of the turret have *Baroque gargoyles* in the shape of dragons' heads.

The vaulted, unadorned staircase, which provides access to both parts of the building, lies to the east of the corridor. The western wooden doors bear the Bishop's

142

insignia, the eastern ones the arms of the Canton of St.Gall; the style is Classical. They were probably made after 1824, when the separation of diocese and canton was complete.

The western palace wing

The former abbot's residence in the western section of the palace wing houses the *Gallus Chapel* on the ground floor, accessible from the fountain courtyard, and above

78 The palace wing from the north. Diagonally to the left, the adjacent New Palace and the abbey church belong to the Late Baroque.

143

is *the residence of the bishop* of the diocese of St.Gall, now reached by the staircase in the east wing of the monastery section. Here the *palace chapel* and a *festival hall* are of chief significance from the point of view of art history. The private rooms, restored in the 1950s, are not accessible.

The Gallus Chapel

The Chapel of the Holy Cross and St.Gallus was established during the time of Abbot Purchart (ruled 958–971) at the spot where, according to tradition, St.Gallus stumbled over a bramble. In the townscape of MEL-CHIOR FRANCK of 1596 we see at this spot a circular building reminiscent of the funeral chapels of medieval

③

79 The Gallus Chapel in the palace wing, consecrated in 1671. Paintings probably by Johann Sebastian Hersche.

saints. This chapel was demolished in 1666 and rebuilt as part of the new palace wing. The new chapel was consecrated in 1671, reappointed, in part, in 1876, and restored in 1958 under ALBERT BAYER. Since the 19th century it has served as a baptismal chapel in place of the Chapel of the Guardian Angels, which had also been used as a baptismal chapel and was demolished in 1807. The accessories of 1876 were removed in 1958, except for the baptismal font.

The restored entrance of the fountain courtyard side is flanked by two larger than life *sandstone statues* of St.Maurice and St.Desiderius. They were made by JOHANN JAKOB OECHSLIN in 1844 and stood, as replacements of the Baroque originals, at the frontispiece of the tower front of the Cathedral, but were replaced by copies in 1934. The greatest treasure in the almost square chapel is an extensive *series of paintings depicting scenes from the life of St.Gallus.* Of the total of 24 pictures (two were lost in 1876), eight are on the walls and 16 on the ceiling. The Latin legends to the pictures, accompanied by relevant Bible quotations, were freely adapted from the *Life of Gallus* written by Walahfried Strabo in 833/34. The pictures show us the saint, his companions and interlocutors, both in open natural surroundings and against architectural backgrounds with perspectives. Their author was very probably the St.Gallen court painter JOHANN SEBASTIAN HERSCHE. In 1760 JOSEF WANNENMACHER reworked the pictures, which produced a curious tension between the strict High Baroque composition of the pictures and the Late Baroque style of painting with its dark, muted colours. Certain scenes show a remarkable ressemblance to the small cartouches depicting the monastic disciplines in the Library, which are the work of Wannenmacher (p.110f.).

In view of the iconographic importance of this Gallus series, we give here the legends to the paintings in full.

1. Presentation of the boy Gallus. «The parents of St.Gallus, devout before God, of high status before the world, indeed kings of Ireland, bring their son, in the flower of his childhood, to be taught by St.Columban. Walahfrid, Chap. 1.» «He will yield fruit early. Psalm 1,3.» – *2. Gallus being taught by Columban.* «St.Gallus, a youth with good aptitudes, grew very virtuously and absorbed worldly works and divine scriptures with such enthusiasm that he was able to bring forth new and old ideas from his resources. Chap. 1.» «By his knowledge he will justify many. Jes. 53,11.» – *3. He is received by King Sigisbert.* «After St.Gallus had gone to Britain and Gaul with Columban and his companions to convert the heathen, he was received by King Sigisbert and asked not to wander further to other peoples. Chap. 2.» «He glorified him in the presence of kings. Eccl. 45,3.» – *4. Destruction of the idols in Tuggen.* «St.Gallus, armed with the zeal of piety, sets fire to the heathen temple in Tuggen and smashes the idols, thus rousing the fury of the heathens, who drive him out from that region. Chap. 4». «I will curse him that curses thee. Gen. 12,3.» – *5. Gallus at Bregenz on Lake Constance.* «After St.Gallus had flung the idols into the lake at Bregenz, he overcame the persecution of demons, because he did not cease to invoke the name of God. Chap. 7.» «The name of the Lord is his hope. Psalm 39,5.» – *6. Missing picture.* It probably represented the leavetaking of Gallus, who remained behind, from Columban, who continued on – an event which was of decisive importance for the establishment of St.Gall. – *7. From Arbon to St.Gall.* «Because St.Gallus wishes to spend the remaining days of his life in solitude, he seeks, under the direction of the deacon Hiltibold, a place in the wilderness suitable for human habitation. Chap. 10.» «They ate manna in the desert. John 6,31.» – *8. Gallus in the brambles.* «St.Gallus catches his foot in dense brambles, falls to the ground on the plateau and in foreknowledge choses this plateau as the residence

146

appointed for him by Heaven. Chap. 11.» «This is my rest for ever. Psalm 131,14.» – *9. Missing picture.* This picture must have shown the setting up of the cross and the consecration of the spot by Gallus after his fall, described by Wahlafried in chapter 11. Fortunately, this scene is also shown in the altarpiece. – *10. Gallus in nocturnal prayer.* «St.Gallus orders the bear to gather wood and bring it to the fire, and, together with the snakes, wild animals and demons, to leave the valley forever. Chap. 11.» «Even the animals listen to him. Judith 11,5.» – *11. Clearing of the forest.* «St.Gallus, who came into this solitude in the year of our Lord 614, in the 85th year of his life, together with his disciples, began to clear the forest and to cultivate the place. Chap. 13.» «The wilderness will rejoice and blossom. Jes 35,1.». – *12. Construction of the monastery.* «While St.Gallus was building the cell and the prayerhouse with his own hands and those of God, the amazing growth of a board was a miraculous prelude to the future flourishing of his monastery. Chaps. 13 and 27.» «God gave the increase. I Cor. 3,6.» – *13. Gallus the teacher.* «In order to endow his monastery with equity, discipline and knowledge, St.Gallus imparts to the deacon John and subsequently several other brothers the monastic way of life and an understanding of the Holy Scriptures. Chap. 20.» «He bestowed upon him the law of life. Sir. 17,11.» – *14. Gallus as healer.* «St.Gallus frees Fridiburga, the daughter of the Alemann Duke Gunzo; as a punishment for doing injustice to the saint, she was possessed by the evil spirit, from which two bishops had vainly tried to liberate her. Chaps. 16 and 18.» «Do good to those who hate you! Luke 6,28.» – *15. Gallus the almsgiver.* St.Gallus distributes to the poor in Arbon the rich presents which he received from the duke as thanks offerings for freeing his daughter, and exhorts his disciples to give alms. Chap. 19.» «Give, and it shall be given unto you. Luke 6,38.» – *16. Presentation of the royal document.* «In order to give thanks to her liberator, Fridiburga obtains from her betrothed, King Sigisbert, that Gallus permanently possess the place inhabited by him, by royal dispensation. Chap. 21.» «Every place whereon the soles of your feet shall tread shall be yours. Deut. 11,24.» – *17. Robing of the bride of God.* «On the day of the wedding celebration, Fridiburga, who followed the counsel of St.Gallus in all things, joins herself to God, whereupon the king, not without tears, yields his bride to the highest suitor. Chap. 22.» «She will be happier if she remains as she is. I Cor. 7.40.» – *18. Election of a bishop in Constance.* «St.Gallus refuses the position of bishop in Constance and proposes that his disciple John be raised to the status of bishop. Although the latter flees such an honour, he is ultimately – although reluctantly and against his will – consecrated. Chap. 24.» «I have chosen to be small in the house of God. Psalm 83,11.» – *19. Miraculous catch of fish.* «Although his guests found nothing to eat in his poor cell, St.Gallus serves them abundantly with fish, wine and flour, which God miraculously provided. Chap. 28.» «Do not be anxious. Matthew 6,34.» – *20. Funeral rites for Columban.* «St.Gallus, informed of the death of his teacher, Columban, by divine inspiration, performs the sacrifice of salvation for his soul and receives his crosier through St.Magnus. Chap. 26.» «Thy staff comforted me. Psalm 22,4.» – *21. Last sermon in Arbon.* «On the feast of St.Michael, St.Gallus lifts up the hearts of his listeners with the grace of his sermon; like the dying swang, he sang more sweetly in the throes of death and spoke his last 'I have spoken'. Chap. 29.» «Do not depart from the words of my mouth! Proverbs 5,7.» – *22. Demise of Gallus.* «After completing 95 years of life, St.Gallus gives up his meritorious soul devoted to the eternal truths, causing Bishop John enormous grief. Chap. 29.» «In death his deeds were marvellous. Eccl. 48,14.» – *23. Return home to St.Gall.* «Since St.Gallus could not be buried in Arbon, he was brought, in a miraculous spectacle, by untamed horses into his holy hermitage, while the candles at his bier continued to burn. Chap. 33.» «He has desired it for his habitation. Pslam 131,13.» – *24. Angel choirs at the grave of Gallus.* «Two alternating choirs of singing angels honour the grave of St.Gallus with heavenly hymns, while two guardian spirits replace the cover spread out over the altar tomb, half burnt by a fallen candle. Book of Miracles, Chap. 4.» «His grave will be glorious. Jes. 11,10.» – *25. Punishment of the thief.* «Count Victor of Chur wishes to remove the body of St.Gallus, which shines radiantly as a result of inumerable miracles, by stealing it from the hermitage, but he is held back by a divine apparition, thrown from his horse and brought home with a broken

80 The 17th picture in the «Life of Gallus» series shows Fridiburga before Gallus; in the background she bids farewell to King Sigisbert.

149

hip. Book of Miracles, Chaps. 12 and 13.» «Spoil not his resting place! Proverbs 24,15.» – *26. The saving of the supplicant.* «St.Gallus protects the wanderer, overcome by sleep, from the unfaithful companion, because he had previously asked the saint's protection by making the sign of the cross and placing himself in his care with these few words: 'St.Gallus, watch over me'. Book of Miracles, Chap. 23.» «A faithful friend is a sturdy shelter. Eccl. 6,14.»

The altar is a retable framed in black, with a pair of columns decorated with flowers in the Baroque style; the main parts probably date from the 17th century. The painting shows the fall of St.Gallus in the brambles, the work of JOSEF WANNENMACHER or a South-German painter akin to him, about 1760.

The Palace Chapel

The private chapel of the bishop, formerly of the abbot, is situated on the first floor exactly above the Gallus Chapel and, like the latter, was consecrated in 1671. Access is through the internal corridor. On the outer side, the door has perforated door jambs crowned with semicircular arches, with mitre, crosier and cross standing out in relief; on the inner side, red-marbled framing columns; on the lintel is the inscription «Electus Dei Gallus dixit: vere Dominus est in Loco isto Vita S.Galli X.VI.» (Gallus, chosen by God, said: Verily at this spot the Lord is present.) According to tradition, this was the spot where Gallus stumbled over a bramble and subsequently built a cell. The square room has a white-painted coffered ceiling with ribbed radiating shapes in a repeat pattern and pâte cuite lily reliefs, like Wessobrunner stucco in wood. The nine octagonal pictures are of *Benedictines particularly honoured* at St.Gall, and the 16 oval pictures show pairs of putti heads. The pictures, painted on linen, are in excellent condition. They can without any doubt be attributed to the St.Gall palace painter JOHANN SE-

81 The palace chapel, today the private chapel of the bishop, is situated above the Gallus Chapel and was consecrated in 1671.

BASTIAN HERSCHE, about 1670. From east to west: – *1. Iso with a receptacle for consecrated oil.* Inscription: «Dedit illi virtutem et potestatem, ut curaret omnem languorem et infirmitatem. Matt. 10. Luc. 9». (He gave him power and authority to cure all melancholia and disease.) Iso (d. 871) was, after Ekkehard, the most learned monk of St. Gall and was also a healer. – *2. Eusebius with a scythe,* holding his severed head in his hands. Inscription: «Tu Dne gloria mea et exaltans caput meum. Psal. 3» (Thou, oh Lord, art my glory and the lifter of my head). The Irishman Eusebius came to the monastery of St. Gall in the 9th century and from there went on to a hermitage on the Viktorberg in the Vorarlberg, where, according to legend, he was murdered. – *3. Tuotilo painting the Virgin.* Inscription: «Implevi eum spiritu Dei Sapientia, Intelligentia, et Scientia in omni opere. Exod. 31» (I have filled him with the spirit of God, with intelligence and knowledge for all works of art). The section of the

151

Bible relating to Bezaleel perfectly fits the St.Gall monk Tuotilo (d. after 912), who was proficient in all the arts and has been shown to be the author of the ivory tablets (Codex 53) in the Library. The painting type is reminiscent of the usual representation of St.Luke. – *4. Otmar with a cask and paten.* Inscription: «Quam pulchra est casta generatio cum claritate. Sap. C. 4» (How beautiful is a chaste generation shining with virtue). Otmar introduced the Benedictine rule into the Gallus cell and was the first abbot (from 719 to 759). The small barrel refers to the miracle of the wine when the body of Otmar was brought back from the island of Werd in the Rhine, across Lake Constance to St.Gall. The consecrated wafers were said to have been found in 864 on the occasion of the opening of the tomb in the Chapel of St.Peter in St.Gall. In 867 his grave was transferred to a church specifically erected in his honour, to the west of the Gallus church. – *5. St.Gallus with the bear.* Inscription: «Ecce ego et pueri mei, quos dedit mihi Dominus. Isa.C.8» (Behold, I and my children, whom the Lord has given me). Gallus appears as the main figure in the centre of the room. In about 612 he built the first monastic cell in the Steinachtal. – *6. Notker in combat with the Devil.* Inscription: «Vas electionis est mihi iste, ut portet nomen meum. Act.C.9» (He is a chosen instrument of mine to proclaim my name). Ekkehard IV wrote of Notker the Stammerer (d. 912), a native of Jonschwil, that he was a vessel of the Holy Ghost such as had never been known. Notker was a poet, teacher and ascetic. According to legend, he gave combat to the Devil in the form of a dog, in the crypt of the abbey church. He was venerated in the monastery as a saint. – *7. Hermann the Lame with a crutch and a globe.* Inscription: «Super salutem et speciem dilexi illam et proposui pro luce habere illam. Sap.7» (More than health and beauty he loved her [Wisdom] and preferred her to the light of day). Hermanus Contractus (d. 1054) was a monk at Reichenau. Although

82 Tuotilo painting the Virgin. Ceiling medallion in the palace chapel, probably by Johann Sebastian Hersche, after 1671.

lame from birth, he was a great mathematician and poet. Among other things, he wrote the antiphony to the Blessed Virgin Mary «Salve Regina», the opening words of which issue from the mouth of the figure. – *8. Monk, presenting two eyes in a book.* Inscription: «Dominus illuminatio mea et salus mea. Psal. 26» (The Lord is my light and my salvation). The reference here is most probably to the monk Victor, venerated in St.Gall, whose eyes were put out outside the monastery and who died in 960 in the hermitage of Viktorsberg (Vorarlberg) (see also the representation in the cupola of the Cathedral, (p.72). – *9. Monk with a skull.* Inscription: «Sancta et salubris

153

83 *Fleeing mastiff with two crosiers. Detail of the Regency stucco work in the festival hall of the bishop's residence, 1730.*

est cogitatio pro defunctis exornare. 2 Macc.12» (It is a holy and healthy thought to pray for the dead). The skull may refer to the St.Gall recluse Hartker, who, between 986 and 1017, wrote and illuminated a two-volume antiphonary (Library, mss. 390/391). The simple altar arrangement with the Pieta painting dates from the early 19th century. The window to the corridor is framed by a credence table with superstructure. At the sides along the wall are *Late Gothic statuettes* of about 1500, representing St.Stephen and St.Laurence.

Unfortunately, in 1958 the wall stucco with reed-like cartouches was removed. It was the work of HANS JOERG HAGGENMUELLER of Kempten in the Allgäu and Brother SERGIUS GNEPLER of Wangen.

On the *third floor* a *festival hall* takes up the entire depth of the palace wing and the space in the corner turrets. The cavetto vault ceiling has *Regency stucco decorations* of 1730, which are arranged to form a cross whose arms converge on the circular central picture. The interlacing ornamentation typical of the time is enriched by acanthus tendrils and branches of flowers. In the corners at the end of the cross there are four reliefs with motifs from the arms of Abbot Josephus von Rudolphi, who commissioned the work; above the oriel, the monastery bear with two mitres refers to the twin monasteries of St.Gall and St.Johann in the Thurtal; on the east side, a stag from the coat of arms of Rudolphi; on the south, the Lamb of God, the arms of St.Johann; on the west, a fleeing mastiff (barony of Toggenburg) with two crosiers, ㉝ probably referring to the Toggenburg war of 1712. The stucco artist, who came from Munich, was perhaps no less than EGID QUIRIN ASAM (1692–1750).

The central *ceiling picture,* painted on linen, shows St.Benedict, accompanied by St.Gallus and St.Otmar, surmounted by a picture of the Mother of God and Sts. Desiderius and Maurice, whose relics had been brought to St.Gall by Gallus. At the foot is a very beautiful perspective of the monastery buildings as they were before the Late Baroque construction. The artist is unknown. The parquet floor, restored in 1958, has a star figure in the centre, which was part of the old floor.

The art collection (no access)
The diocesan art collection and the continually increasing collection of works of art belonging to the Catholic Church bring together *important individual works* of heterogeneous provenance. The basis of the collection goes back to Bishop Karl Greith (reigned 1862–1882). The collection is weighted towards *Late Gothic panel paintings.* Particularly worth mentioning are the large volets from the former high altar in the Convent of St.Katharinenthal in the Canton of Thurgau, of about 1480; a small altar-piece with volets from the Convent of Rorschach, dating from the second quarter of the 15th century; another from the former monastery of Rueti, in the Canton of Zurich (subsequently in the monastery of

Wurmsbach), of 1513, and two Renaissance reredos from Messkirch, of about 1530, as well as individual pictures, including a Holy Family by HANS SCHAEUFFELIN, 1513. Among the *Baroque pictures* should be mentioned a sketch for a ceiling painting for the church of Seitingen (Wuerttemberg), by FRANZ LUDWIG HERRMANN, 1759, and a sketch for a painting for an altar-piece in the monastery of Zwettl, by PAUL TROGER, 1734/35, as well as a small oil-painting of 1786 by JANUARIUS ZICK, showing Notker's combat with the Devil. In addition, the collection contains numerous Late Gothic and Baroque *sculptures,* and in recent years, 16th and 17th-century *cabinet panels* which have some link with the monastery of St.Gall have also been added.

84 *Eastern palace wing. Corridor on the second floor with doors leading to the dining room and former guest rooms (now offices).*

85 The monastery buildings shortly before the Late Baroque transformations. Stucco work in the Dining-room by Andreas Bentele, 1752/53.

The Eastern Palace Wing

The ground floor consists of vaulted rooms which take up the entire depth of the building.

The first and second floors have vaulted corridors ⑧⑤ on the side which looks onto the monastery square. The former cells and guest rooms (now offices) lie to the south. The wooden *door frames* with columns recall the monastic period. Except for the *Dining-room* on the sec-

157

ond floor (no. 200), there are no state rooms. A Baroque wall safe with an elaborate lock in room no. 101 and panelling of 1895 depicting historical scenes in room no. 105 should not be overlooked.

The Dining-room

The former Dining-room for the abbot's guests was decorated in 1752/53 by ANDREAS BENTELE of Lindau with artificial marble, and a stucco-work ceiling. The rectangular room, with its five lines of windows, is of unique beauty. Instead of panelling, colourful *breasting made of false marble* lines the room in soft waves and upturned cornices.

The individual sections are decorated with yellow, red and blue marbled colours. On the long corridor side there are two (new) doors, surmounted by architraves with rocaille, between which is the former *abbot's seat* (?) with curving Rococo surmounts. The parquet floor of oak and maple is laid in a chequer-board pattern with cropped corners. Two corner stoves made by the stovefitter SCHLAPFER of Rorschach are missing. The ceiling has outstanding *Rococo stucco decoration.* In the centre, in the place where the monastery arms were formerly, are the arms of the Canton of St.Gall, accompanied at the foot by two putti dressed as warriors, and at the sides by two putti with wheatsheaves and a book, probably symbolizing the occupations of soldiery, farming and teaching. In the eastern field is a *relief of the monastery of St.Gall* before the alterations made in the 18th century, and in the western field the monastery of Neu St.Johann. In the transverse field are personifications of Justice with a sword and scales, and of Wisdom with a mirror and serpent; in the corners, the four seasons (clockwise): a woman crowned with a garland of flowers (spring), a man with a sickle, rake and wheatsheaf (summer), a putto with grapes (autumn), and a putto as a hunter with game (winter).

158

The artificial marble, which is scarcely ever found in such bold colours and forms, is particularly impressive. ANDREAS BENTELE also made the side altars in the parish church of Bregenz in 1750 and those in the church of Lindau in 1754.

In the windows are *glass paintings,* presented to the Canton of St.Gall in 1953 on the occasion of its 150th anniversary; four of these are by AUGUST WANNER and one by ULRICH HAENNY, both from the town of St.Gall.

86 *The Dining-room in the eastern palace wing. Artificial marble and ceiling stucco work by Andreas Bentele, 1752/53.*

The New Palace (Neue Pfalz)

The palace was the official residence of the abbot. (The German name «Pfalz» comes from the Latin «palatium» [palace] and goes back to the imperial palaces of the Middle Ages.) Since ancient times, the residence of the abbot lay outside the enclosure, east of the church, that is to say approximately in the centre of the present-day monastery square. It was only during the time of Abbot Diethelm Blarer (ruled 1530–1564) that the «household» in the north-east corner of the monastery area was built; it was replaced in 1666 by the present palace wing containing the Bishop's residence (p.141). On the evidence ⑦ of a sketch made after 1709, the medieval buildings around the present monastery square were a stone complex with eaves, several floors, and groups of Gothic windows. A coach-house adjoined it on its south side.

Prince-Abbot Beda Angehrn had the new palace, the present administration building, built in 1767–1769. The master builder was JOHANN FERDINAND BEER. IGNAZ WILHELM of Schlachters (Kreis Lindau) and MARTIN FRYRLE of Goldach near St.Gall were engaged as master carpenters. By 1769 the building had a roof and the internal construction was completed. It was decorated only gradually. The private apartments of the abbot were painted in 1771/72 by ANTONI DICK of Isny and his son. The high point of the decoration of the inside of the building was the ornamentation in 1786/87 of the so-called *throne room* on the top floor of the central projection, where the worldly power of the abbot found expression. However, it was also in this room that Mueller-Friedberg proclaimed the *independent canton of St.Gall* in 1803.

After the abolition of the position of prince-abbot in 1805 and the separation of the monastery's possessions

87 Monastery square from the west. Palace wing (right) of 1666, New Palace 1767–69, north wing 1838–41 and Children's Chapel 1843–46.

between Church and State in 1813, the new palace became the seat of the Administration of the Canton of St.Gall. As a consequence of the new building's new role, the artwork from the time of the monastery rapidly disappeared, and not even the room decorations in Historicism style were spared. In the south-east corner on the third floor was the «relief room», so called because it contained a large relief of the Canton of St.Gall, made in 1845–54 by CARL AUGUST SCHOELL (1820–1878); it was shown at the Great Exhibition in Paris in 1855. Schoell's model was later placed in the Cantonal School and was recently destroyed because of lack of space. The Pompeian-type murals in the relief room, painted in 1850 by DAVID ALOIS SCHMID (1791–1861) of Schwyz, met with a similar fate. The only parts that were kept were the landscape views which provide a glimpse beyond the cantonal boundaries: «Ragaz with Grisons

161

scenery, Weesen with the steambout «Spluegen» and the Glarus lowlands, Brunnen with Lake Uri and Ruetli, Rapperswil with Lake Zurich, confluence of the Thur with the Rhine at Flaach, Weissbad with Alpine ibex, Lake Constance at Kreuzlingen and Constance. The other pictures were destroyed. In 1881/82 the former throne room, now the Great Council Chamber, in the central projection underwent a complete *transformation in Historicism style.* Since then, numerous changes have been introduced, both inside and outside, some of them very recently. For example, the window shutters are missing at present. However, the Baroque style of the building as a whole remains largely intact.

The new palace is a four-storeyed building, of symmetrical lines, which symbolically closes off the monastery square to the east. The *central projection,* with its four giant sandstone pilasters and mansard roof, binds together the great mass of the building and forms a secular counterpart to the ascending twin-towered facade of the Cathedral. In the centre an archway connects through to the Charles Borromeo Gate and the former coachhouse (now a theatre). Instead of the former abbey emblem, the apex of the western arch bears arms of the Canton of St.Gall, marked 1803, encircled by garlands and surmounted by vases. In the passageway are three doors, that to the south wing Classical, to the north wing neo-Baroque, and a modern one made by the architect RO-BERT BAMERT in 1981. Below the entire length and depth of the new palace lie imposing *cellars* with tunnel vaults and lunettes. The pilasters correspond to the corridor running above. In the projection they are paired like triumphal arches. The upper floors are reached by a *staircase* in the north-east corner of the central projection. The cast-iron bannisters and the wooden handrail decorated at the ends with animal heads are worth noting. There are secondary staircases in the corners. The four *vaulted corridors* lie – in contrast to the palace wing

⑧⑧

162

88 Animal heads ending the hand rails on the staircase in the New Palace, about 1770.

– away from the square on the east side. The perforated, brown-grained *door frames* are another reminder of the time of the monastery. On the ground floor, where the Foundation Archives and the State Archives were kept until 1978, the adjoining rooms are vaulted and the windows have grilles. Otherwise, the offices have flat ceilings and only a few have been left as they were originally.

At the time of the monastery, the central projection already housed the abbey administration centre and the throne room. After the establishment of the cantonal administration in 1805, the three powers of the state were housed here: on the first floor, the *Cantonal Tribunal,* on the second floor the scat of *Government,* and on the third the *Great Council* (Cantonal Parliament). The former courtroom (today the Financial Office) is distinguished on the corridor side by magnificent *double doors* with Rococo carvings. Two similar but smaller doors lead to ⁸⁹

163

the Administrative Council Chamber decorated in modern style, and to a side-room (now a reading room). In the corridors on the first and second floors are *portraits of the Landammanns* (the title of the cantonal president)

89 *New Palace. Door in Rococo style, on the first floor, about 1770.*

of the 20th century, some of them by well-known St.Gall artists, such as WILLY FRIES, AUGUST WANNER, FERDINAND GEHR, etc.

The Great Council Chamber (Parliamenthall)

After the Canton of St.Gall was established in 1803, the Great Council met early on in the so-called throne room of the abbot, situated in the central projection. The engraver JOHANN BAPTIST ISENRING (1796–1860) depicted the session of the constitutional council of 14 January 1831 in an aquatint.

On 19 November 1879 the Cantonal Parliament decided to renovate the chamber in such a way as to preserve the decorations, «of true artistic merit». The St.Gall architect JOHANN CHRISTOPH KUNKLER was assigned to the project. His plan, now in the State Archives, shows – below the painted walls and the cavetto vault ceiling – a seating arrangement turned to the west and a U-shaped gallery with columns jutting forward in the eastern part of the chamber. The project did not meet with the approval of the Great Council because of the unfavourable positioning of the seating, against the light, and also because the monastic Baroque no longer suited this period of cultural transition nor the self-image of the Canton of St.Gall.

On 5 March 1881, the cantonal architect THEODOR GOHL (1844–1910) submitted a project for complete rebuilding, which envisaged a seating arrangement facing north and a platform to the south. Before an agreement was reached, ALBERT MUELLER (1846–1912), of Zurich, KASPAR EMIL STUDER (1844–?) of Winterthur and EUGEN FALLER (1846–1900) of St.Gall were consulted for their expertise. The entire rebuilding took place the same year, 1881, at a cost of 30,000 francs. The stucco decoration was carried out by the Zurich firm of DELLA TORRE UND GREPPI, and the painting by the St.Gall artist DANIEL FRIEDRICH KIRCHHOFER (1831–1885). The heraldry consultant was the painter and armorial connoisseur CHRISTIAN BUEHLER (1825–1898) of Nesslau, who, in Berne, looked after the painting collections of the city and of the confederacy. Because of poor eyesight, he refused the assignment as a whole, but produced the cartoons for the coats of arms. These cartoons are preserved in the State Archives.

Almost 100 years later, in 1979/80, the Great Council Chamber was restored under the direction of ROBERT BAMERT of the architectural firm of Mueller und Bamert in St.Gall. The paintings, in the Historicism style, were restored by JOHANN HEROVITS of Goldach, and RINO FONTANA of Jona, and the furniture was also restored, some pieces of the older furniture being re-used. The foyer with steps to the platform was given a new look. The adjoining rooms on the south side, the Conference Room and the Council Chamber were returned to their Late Baroque or Classical appearance.

⑨⁰ *The original Throne Room*
The festival hall, where the prince-abbot received the delegations of the empire, of the cantons of the confederacy and of his subjects, was a highly individual testimonial to secular decoration. The Late Baroque illusionist painting was the work of the Tyrolean master JOSEF ANTON PULLACHER (1737–1799) of Telfs, who, two years later, on an assignment from Abbot Beda Angehrn, 1787, produced the ceiling paintings which are still extant in the parish church of Niederhelfenschwil. Of the painted decoration of the Baroque throne room, coloured copies have been preserved, made at the request of the Society for the Promotion of the Fine Arts shortly before the destruction of the paintings in 1881. The transition style between the Baroque and Louis XVI ties in with the great tradition of illusionist architectural painting since ANDREA POZZO, but it also has a rustic component with

theatrical effects, such as are found in the painting of the Tyrol, the home of the artist, Pullacher.

The following is a *description* of the room shortly before it was rebuilt, written by J. Ludwig Meyer, who also photographed it:

When we enter the room, we find ourselves in an open, airy hall, with slender columns with red-brown marble shafts on which highlights play merrily and which stand out strongly with heavy shadows from the yellowish-green wall. A richly moulded, widely projecting beam, resting on Ionic bronze capitals with hanging festoons, divides the building into two parts horizontally by its overhang. The wall is broken up by windows, doors and niches, the bluish-red casings of which furnish an agreeable contrast to the green of the wall, and which are animated and decorated with festoons of fruit of all kinds, medallions and small trees in red and white pots, the colourful fruit of which reach out temptingly towards the observer. On each long side we look out through a broad arch into the open beyond, where Ceres and Flora, Neptune and Hercules invite the observer into green pergolas. Various fountains send their jets into the air and behind them one sees far into the pastel-co-

90 *Former throne room in the New Palace. Copy of the wall paintings of 1787 by Josef Anton Pullacher, destroyed in 1881.*

loured landscape, over shady groves, beyond a proud watchtower, along fertile expanses with a town and houses, up to the faintly indicated far away mountains, which disappear into a sky made pink by the setting sun. From the above-mentioned beam rises powerful stonework, animated by mouldings and projections, the greenish-yellow surfaces of which are decorated with heavy golden fruit festoons and rosettes. In the centre a broad shallow arch breaks up the stonework, and a balustrade with short brown columns encircles, like a crown, the great fantasy building, spanned by the lightly clouded sky. Within the arch is grouped, around a gable-like central part, a variety of green bushes, cacti, fig trees and other small trees and flowers of all kinds, arranged in vivid and attractive alternation, and made particularly lively by delightful putti, blond and red-headed, almost nude little fellows, holding tendrils, parasols and other objects, who represent the seasons. On each of the four sides, breaking up the balustrade in the centre, is a crowning oval shield containing the four quarters of the arms of the prince-abbot, the bear, the mastiff, the Lamb of God and the arms of the Angehrn family, which display the red ermine cloak, the sword, the crosier and all the insignia of the prince-abbot's power. In the south-east corner the sun rises radiantly and, facing it, the pale-yellow crescent of the moon hides behind the clouds; two doves have alighted on the balustrade and bill and coo unconcerned by the eagle hovering with outspread wings high in the skies above carrying in his beak the lantern, a masterpiece of Venetian cut-glass. White curved furniture with gilded moulding and various decorations animates the room, and it must have been a lively and colourful scene when Prince-Abbot Beda, in his rich vestments, surrounded by the brothers of his order in their black habits, received the deputies of his subjects and the delegates of the cantons and of the empire in their colourfully embroidered robes, with the daggers and the chains of the Orders. – *Anzeiger fuer Schweizerische Altertumskunde 16* (1883), p.375ff.

The present Great Council Chamber

The rhomboidal chamber, which takes up the entire depth of the projection, is spanned by a flat coffered ceiling and illuminated by ten segmental arch windows. The seating, arranged facing north towards the presidential platform in the manner of an arena, the elegant wall and ceiling decoration and the colourful painting decor in neo-Renaissance style provide a *ceremonial atmosphere,* befitting a place where important political decisions are taken. The walls with their paired and single pilasters match on each side. The triple front with the presidential seat and side entrances has its counterpart in the double-storeyed gallery with observers' platform and press tribune. The coffered, painted stucco ceiling is divided geometrically into a middle field and side fields, framed by chains of pearl and egg-and-dart and acanthus mouldings. Its *being painted* in a colour palette of pastel grisaille, ranging from green and blue to an intense red, especially enhances the atmosphere. On the walls heraldic and political subjects are depicted, on the ceiling allegorical and didactic ones.

Above the windows are ten *medallions with the coats of arms of the old dominions,* which were united with the

91 Great Council Chamber in the New Palace, view towards the observer gallery. Decorated in Historicism style, 1881/82, restored in 1979/80.

present Canton of St.Gall in 1803. They are accompanied by texts, as follows: *In the western part of the projection:* 1. ALTE LANDSCHAFT ST.GALLEN (Old Territory of St.Gall): On a gold ground, a standing bear with red ears and tongue, holding a brown tree branch in both paws. – GRAFSCHAFT TOGGENBURG (County of Toggenburg): On a gold ground, a standing black mastiff with red tongue and silver collar. After 1468 the land along the Thur and the Necker belonged to the abbey of St.Gall. 3. STADT RAPPERSWIL (Town of Rapperswil): On a silver ground, two red roses flecked with gold, with green sepals, on red stalks. Since 1458 this town on the upper part of Lake Zurich had been a protectorate of the confederacy. 2. GRAFSCHAFT UTZNACH (County of Utznach): On a red ground, above three green peaks, a double rose flecked with gold, on a green stem, with green sepals and three leaves arranged in an alternating pattern. The former Toggenburg territory on either side of the Ricken had been a confederate bailiwick of Schwyz and Glarus since 1469. 5. HERRSCH(AFT) WINDEGG / LANDSCH(AFT) GASTER (Territory of Windegg / District of Gaster): On a silver ground, a red diagonal band, accompanied by two striding red lions, the bottom one turned to the left. The arms refer to the former territory of the counts of Kyburg, since 1438 a confederate bailiwick of Schwyz and Glarus. *In the eastern part of the projection:* 6. STADT SANCT GALLEN (Town of St.Gall): On a silver ground, a standing black bear with gold armour, gold collar and ears and red tongue. St.Gall had been an independent municipal republic since the Late Middle Ages. 7. LANDSCHAFT RHEINTAL (District of Rheintal): On a gold background, a standing black ibex with red tongue and markings. Since 1490 the land along the lower reaches of the Rhine had been a confederate bailiwick. 8. FREIHERRSCHAFT SAX (Barony of Sax): Fissures of red and gold. The former domain of the barons of Sax became a baili-

(92)

170

92 Great Council Chamber. Arms of the City of Rapperswil, painted in 1882 after a design by Christian Buehler.

wick of Zurich in 1615. 9. GRAFSCHAFT WERDEN-BERG (County of Werdenberg): On a silver ground, a black trilobate church banner on three gold rings, decorated at the bottom with golden flames pointing downwards. The arms refer to the counts of Montfort and of Werdenberg. The central area around Werdenberg had been a bailiwick of Glarus since 1517. 10. GRAF-SCHAFT SARGANS (County of Sargans): On a red background, a silver trilobate church banner on three silver rings, with silver flames pointing downwards. The arms refer to the counts of Montfort and of Sargans. The territory of Sargans had been a confederate bailiwick since 1483 and, by order of Napoleon, was joined to the newly-founded Canton of St.Gall.

The ceiling paintings are a return, in the Historicism style, to the world of figures and *grotesques of the Renaissance,* in the Pompeian colours beloved in the 19th century that can also be seen in the Old Museum in St.Gall, which was completed in 1877. It may be that the artist, Daniel Friedrich Kirchhofer, of whose work these

171

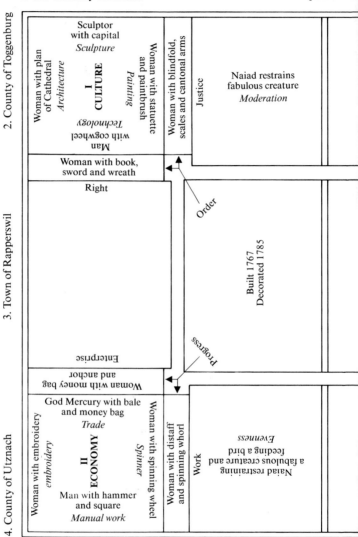

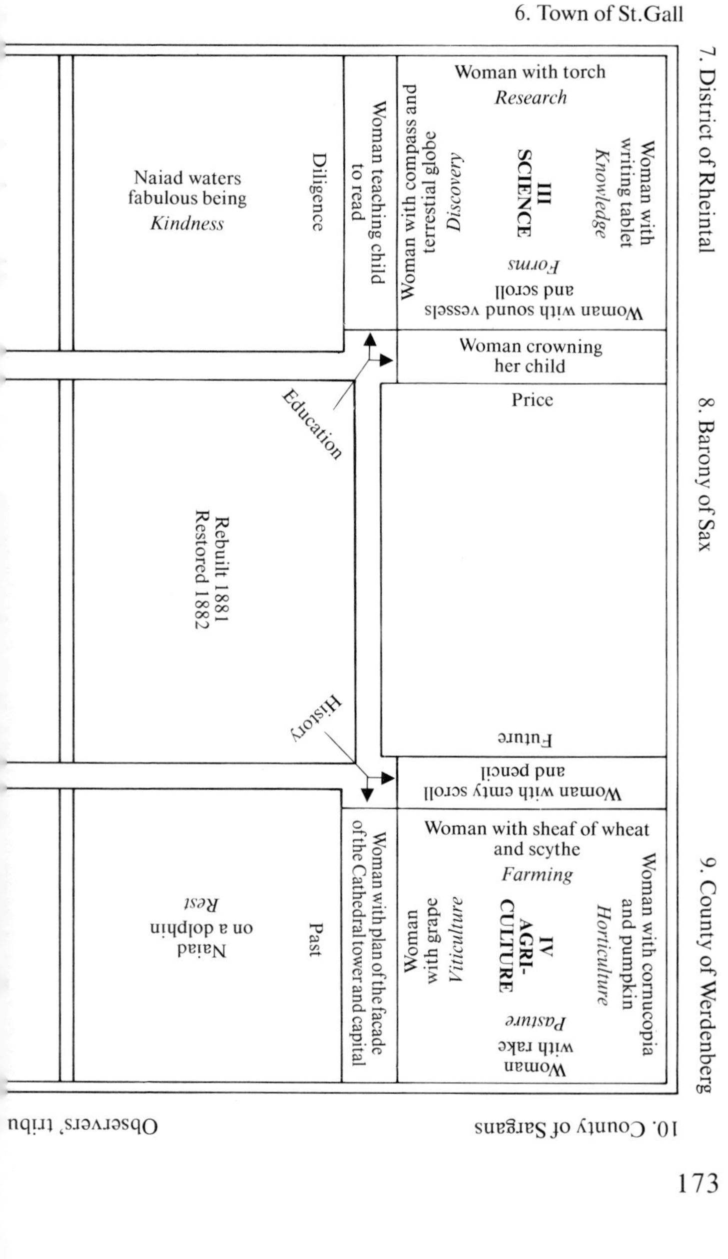
6. Town of St.Gall
7. District of Rheintal
8. Barony of Sax
9. County of Werdenberg
10. County of Sargans
Observers' tribu
Woman with torch
Research
Woman with writing tablet
Knowledge
III
SCIENCE
Woman with compass and terrestial globe
Discovery
Woman with sound vessels and scroll
Forms
Woman teaching child to read
Diligence
Naiad waters fabulous being
Kindness
Woman crowning her child
Education
Price
Rebuilt 1881
Restored 1882
Future
History
Woman with emty scroll and pencil
Woman with sheaf of wheat and scythe
Farming
Woman with cornucopia and pumpkin
Horticulture
IV
AGRI-
CULTURE
Woman with grape
Viticulture
Woman with rake
Pasture
Woman with plan of the facade of the Cathedral tower and capital
Past
Naiad on a dolphin
Rest

monumental paintings are all that is known, based himself on pattern books and tapestry models of the 19th century. He was probably also influenced by the grotesque paintings of RAPHAEL in the loggias of the Vatican. The ornamental bands, arabesques and doves, as well as the damascene ornamentation of the walls, are reminiscent of designs for the contemporary *St.Gall lacework.* The figures echo *antique mythology,* as in the Manuscript Room of the Library (pp.115ff.), and the artist's wit and irony show through in places (see diagram). Unfortunately the individual gods and muses cannot be identified with total certainty.

The four corner sections with figures represent the cornerstones of a well-functioning state. The large female figures in the red grotesque fields personify the «protec-

94 *Great Council Chamber. North-west corner of the ceiling, with allegories to culture as well as to the legal system of the State of St.Gall.*

174

tive spirits» and «virtues» who guarantee prosperity. I. A pre-requisite for *cultural activity* is an orderly state, where justice and law promote a favourable climate. II. A *progressive enonomy* is based on the spirit of enterprise and the work of the citizens, expressed in the Canton of St.Gall in the textile industry especially. III. The young Canton of St.Gall was and still is known for its *purposeful educational policy* at all levels of schooling and of professional training. IV. The *history of St.Gall* is expressed in the radiant buildings of the ecclesiastical precinct and in the belief of the young state in its own future. Balanced agriculture provides a good supply base. ⑨④

The central bands are adorned with fantasy winged beings, naiads and tritons, which are there for decorative effect but must also be iconographical references to political rhetoric in the Parliament. In contrast, the grotesque figures in the friezes of the ceiling and wall pilasters are very difficult to identify.

Unfortunately, in Switzerland, 19th-century wall paintings have only sporadically been studied for their political significance. But in any case, the painting in the Great Council Chamber is an interesting attempt to use profane allegory to symbolize the state, as was done on a large scale a few years later in the parliamentary building of the Bundeshaus in Berne.

To the north of the Great Council Chamber is *a Conference room* (no. 315) *and a Council room* (no. 316). Both rooms have historical significance and were lovingly restored and furnished during the most recent restoration. The Conference room is entered from the corridor through a plain, Classical walnut door; the space above the door lintel is painted on the inside, as are the two side doors, with a still-life and two heroic landscapes of rather modest quality. The walls are covered with a decorative *linen wallpaper,* with colourful late 18th-century painting on a white ground: flower garlands with victory banners, streamers with notes and trumpets, as well as ⑨⑤

175

putti with shawms (oboes) and cornucopias. The themes remind one of the thunderous rumblings of the French Revolution. The adjoining *Council room* has *five doors* with still-lives and imaginary landscapes above the door lintels. Its somewhat simpler and probably more recent *linen wallpaper* has hanging flower garlands in zig-zag form, crossed by a stipple pattern of the «pieds de poules» type. Both wallpapers are probably of Parisian origin.

In the roof space to the south of the Great Council Chamber is the *Crime Museum* (no. 401). This educational collection, used for police training, can be viewed upon preliminary request to the Cantonal Police.

Individual Showpieces
Five particularly precious bureaux, found when the St.Gall Cantonal Administration moved into the new palace in 1803, are now in the offices of heads of departments. They are described below.

1. Bureau in office no. 213 (Head of the Department of Internal Affairs). The basic form is decorated with wavy curves and has a tabernacle-like surmount. The drawers of the lower and upper sections are decorated with floral and zoomorphic intarsia. On the ornamental part of the writing flap there is a wooded landscape with a town and a lake, in the foreground the Good Shepherd, surrounded by sheep, on the right a wolf waiting to pounce. On the narrow doors of the upper section, St.Benedict with crosier and open Book of Rules: «Ad monicionem Pij Patris libenter excite. Ex Prologo S.Regulae» (Take the exhortations of the Good Father seriously.); above the saint, a rising cloud with angels, who carry a mitre and a poison chalice (the attribute of St.Benedict). The niche is lined with flowered paper. On the narrow sides are charming garlands with an owl and

◄ **95** *Conference room in the New Palace. Detail of the painted linen wallpaper from Paris, end 18th century.*

doves. On the sides of the desk: right, a fox, a bear and a wolf, as well as a hare beneath a tree in front of a mountain landscape; left, two monks and a gardener in front of architectural scenery. On the beveled corners of the desk, high reliefs with festoons of flower and fruit, below each is a (Gallus) bear, the one on the left hitting the fruit with a wooden club. The squares of the seat niche depict: left, a hermit reading below a tree; right, a monk with a raised

96 New Palace. Monumental secretary in room No. 220, probably made before 1750.

cross in front of a grotto; and on the front a nobleman in Dutch costume, holding a falcon on his left fist and leading a lion on a chain with his right hand.

Only in this room are the *historical features* still intact. The ceiling has *Rococo stucco work* with a central field and corner cartouches, from about 1770; the floor consists of lozenge-shaped parquet. *The three doors* are framed with bundles of rods wound round with laurels and in the panels are bunches of twigs and rosettes. The fasces motif is reminiscent of the St.Gall cantonal arms and may refer to the establishment of the Canton in 1803.

2. Monumental bureau in room no. 220 (Head of the ⑨⑥ Department of Education). A broad and spacious showpiece, rigidly subdivided, with square-cut corners on the lower section. Two bears serve as the supports at the front and two mastiffs at the back. They and the lamb lying in the centre of the curved footboard are the animals on the coat of arms of the monastery (see stucco ceiling, p.155). The desk credence is stepped and the upper section has a flat stepped gable and black-framed concave curved drawers. All the outer surfaces of the drawers, as well as the writing flap and the sides, are decorated with intarsia: birds of paradise, wild animals, beetles and butterflies, leaf tendrils, flowers and ears of corn, as well as fruit and berries, mixed with romantic landscape scenes. On the left of the sloping writing flap is a lion tamer in Oriental clothes, and on the right, a winged lady with a horn; between them a bunch of flowers lies crosswise. Above this is a broad surface with pictures: left, two manor-houses and to the right of the tree, a bearded drummer, and four riders in French costume killing a bear. The small cupboard door depicts St.Gallus before the Virgin Mary. Inlaid on the upper side of the skirting board are a knife with three small crosses on the blade, a pair of scissors with a small cross, and a clay pipe. These may be the disguised signature of the unknown artist,

179

who must have used knife and scissors. This is most certainly the oldest of the five pieces of furniture, made before 1750.

3. Tabletop commode in room no. 219 (Office of the Department of Education). This is a relatively small piece of furniture. On the front door and on the upper writing flap there is extensive flower ornamentation, otherwise only decorative veneer. On the lower flap, which can be pulled out, is a picture of the body of St.Otmar, laid out with a paten on his breast and the inscription: «HIC HABITABO QUONIAM ELIGI, Psl. 132» (Here will I live, as I have chosen him). The reference is to an event in the year 864, when the coffin of St.Otmar was opened in St.Gall and on the breast of the corpse, pieces of bread (wafers) were found which were still as fresh as on the first day. In the niche of the surmount in a rich Rococo frame is the inscription: «NOVISSIMA HORA EST, 1.Jan.» (On 1 January the year is still very young).

4. Secretary standing on ball-shaped feet in room no. 201 in the palace wing (Head of the Department of Finance). It has a broad lower section with two stacks of convex drawers, a stepped upper section with decorative wings and a curved top. On the drawers, simple veneer and Rococo decorations. On the front of the seat niche, a bird with a ring in its beak, over a fence overgrown with flowers. The writing flap shows St.Gallus' fall into the brambles, with the inscription: «HAEC REQUIES MEA» (Here is my rest, Ps. 151). On the small cupboard door is a virtuoso depiction of the Annunciation, perhaps after an Augsburg engraving; below, the inscription «FIAT» (Thy will be done), the whole encircled by flowers and surmounted by a crown.

5. Slender secretary in room no. 504 (Moosbruggstrasse 11, Head of the Department of National Economy). The low bottom part has concave side sections. The upper part, with a raised centre, is surmounted by ornate roofing. The drawers can be blocked by a central lock within the upper part. The substructure and the seat niche have inlaid bunches of flowers and fruit, also a bird picking at fruit; on the cupboard itself are rocaille cartouches, identical in form. On the inclined writing flap is a landscape with a river, with a sailing boat on the right and a fishing boat on the left, the latter threatened by a disintegrating dragon (a reference to the Devil). In the centre is a tower-like cloud formation with the bearded bust of a saint with pectoral cross of mother-of-pearl. Below the desk a writing flap rests on two arms with lions' heads; on the veneered surface, an elegant complex strip with a central rocaille. On the high cupboard doors are a tower and dragon and the papal insignia, above which is a half-figure of a praying monk, the whole surmounted by a gloriole with a cross, made of mother-of-pearl, as are the hands and face of the monk. The two pictures apparently refer to the hermit Pietro Angelari da Murrone, who was elected pope, as Coelestin V, on 5 September 1294, at the age of 80; shortly afterwards, however, he was deposed by Cardinal Benedetto Caëtani, subsequently Pope Boniface VIII, and he died in prison on 19 May 1296. Coelestin, who was canonized in 1313, was the patron saint of Abbot Coelestin Gugger von Staudach (ruled 1740–1767), to whom the piece ap-

97 Secretary in room No. 504, formerly the private property of Abbot Coelestin Gugger von Staudach. Inlaid writing flap.

181

parently belonged. His ownership is also indicated by a built-in «Gugger» (cuckoo), which can be made to sing by activating a pedal.

Evaluation

The showpieces described here, which were only recently excellently restored by ERNST BERNET of St.Gall, are among the most impressive achievements of the art of cabinet-making in its Late Baroque manifestation in the Canton of St.Gall. A comparison of the style here and in the reliefs, inlay work and sgraffito drawings of the Library leaves no doubt that all five of these masterly pieces are from the *workshop of the monastery of St.Gall,* which was headed by the artistically gifted monastery Brother GABRIEL LOSER (1701–1785). Unfortunately it has not yet been possible to identify the hand of Loser in the output of the workshop, nor do these showpieces reveal the name of their creator. However, it can be said that the decorative intarsia, such as the flower pieces and the abstract decorative elements, reveal a particularly high level of *artistic perfection,* whereas the representations of figures are sometimes awkward and the landscapes even naïve. The cabinet-makers based their work on particular models, some contemporary (religious themes from Augsburg?) and some going back to the 17th century (secular themes and grotesques). The small genre pictures correspond to the style of Late Baroque stove painting (Steckborn, Canton of Thurgau). Pattern books must have been available for the zoological representations. However, in contrast to the artistic development of the Manuscript Room of the Library (p.115), it has not here been possible to trace the direct models.

Cabinet-making requires great *familiarity with the materials* and understanding of the woods used, and also a high level of technical skill for cutting the veneers, engraving, staining and burning, glueing and varnishing. As in the Library, walnut was chiefly used: trunk wood for

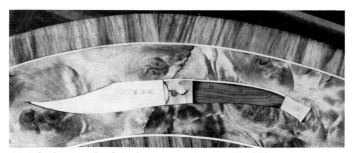

98 *Inlaid carving knife in the secretary in room No. 220.*

the framing herring-bone pattern veneers, veined root wood for the inner surfaces. The often darker filets were apparently burned in sand or stained subsequently. The light coloured picture surrounds (maple?) were incised with sharp knives and, for a sculptural effect, burned with red-hot irons or rubbed with rust. The striking green shading must have been produced by the use of verdigris. Item no. 5 also has mother-of-pearl inlays.

No matter how high the artistic level of the St.Gall workshop, the *monastery of Fischingen* provided very serious competition. Excellent marquetry work can still be seen there, for example on the priests' seats in the Iddakapelle and on the ornamental entrances to the abbot's residence, the dining-room and the library, as well as on individual pieces of 18th-century furniture, in the production of which the sculptor families of FROEHLI and BACHMANN were involved. Apart from genre scenes and floral pieces, the principal themes at Fischingen are contemporary warrior figures and other costumed figures, which, in comparison with St.Gall, are inlaid into brighter and also richer veneer. They ressemble very closely the veneer panels on the second and third floors of the «Baronenhaus» in Wil. It is very possible that for this decoration the owner, Pankraz Gruebler, 1715, no longer turned to St.Gall, but rather to the workshop of the monastery of Fischingen.

183

The North Wing

The initial studies for a horseshoe arrangement of outer monastic buildings goes back to the Einsiedeln architect and monk of St.Gall, CASPAR MOOSBRUGGER, 1721. After the construction of the new palace in 1767–69, the north wing, which had been planned at the same time, remained unbuilt. In 1831/32 the architect FELIX WILHELM KUBLY took up the Baroque building ideas again and at the request of the Catholic Administration Council submitted a project for canonical residences. However, after the cantonal administration dissolved the canonical chapter, the project came to a standstill and was only taken up again in 1836, when it was planned to build a *cantonal arsenal* on the site. Kubly's *new plan,* for an elongated corner building with new access from the Marktgasse to the monastery square, was carried out, with the exception of an additional mezzanine storey, in 1838–41. For this purpose it was necessary to demolish the «wine house» and the stables, both dating back to the time of the monastery, as well as the partition wall that stood behind them. Until 1896 the new wing served as an arsenal, then as the town fire station and as the storehouse for the Cantonal Library. In 1919 and again in 1962 there were competitions for a new building. However, ultimately the administration decided to retain the Kubly building, restoring it on the outside and refurnishing it on the inside, and to widen it with a low addition on the north side. The building contract was awarded to architect ERNEST BRANTSCHEN (b. 1922) and the cantonal master-builder ROLF BLUM; the Federal expert, ALBERT KNOEPFLI, was responsible for looking after the historical aspects.

The three-storeyed, L-shaped building with 21 windows facing the square and nine facing the Marktgasse,

99 *Central part of the north (or arsenal) wing, built by Felix Wilhelm Kubly, 1838–41; in front, Baroque fountain.*

which leads into the square, has the features of the Florentine Early Renaissance typical of *Munich Historicism.* Its direct precursor was the Munich Staatsbibliothek by FRIEDRICH GAERTNER (1792–1847), built in 1832–43. Characteristic of this style are the rusticated plinth storey with three central portals and two additional side portals at each end of the building. The storeys are sharply separated by a continuous moulding. At the corners are rusticated lesenes and below the roof projection a console rim. The portals and the round-arch windows in the upper storeys are surmounted by ornamental bosses. The gently sloping saddleback roof has small dormer windows, amounting to 18 on both sides. The *flat-roofed addition on the north side* in exposed concrete is modern in form, but is clearly subordinate to the building as a whole. The north front has lamelliform windows and the reading room situated behind receives light from above through sawtooth windows.

The north wing, which has been entirely rebuilt on the inside, now contains three important cultural institutes: *the Abbey Archives, the State Archives and the Cantonal Administration Library,* as well as an *exhibition hall, the Cantonal Tribunal* and other *administrative departments.* The visitors' entrance is in the centre of the side that looks onto the square, near the fountain. The entrance hall, lit by three arcade windows on the north side, has ornamental ceiling paintings by FERDINAND GEHR (b. 1894) of Altstaetten. On the right is a painted door, by WALTER BURGER (b. 1923) of Berg, which opens into the spacious exhibition hall. On the left a staircase leads to the service areas below. In the atrium is a bronze sculpture by MAX OERTLI (b. 1921) of St.Gall, and in the reading room a marble fountain by FREDI THALMANN (b. 1939) of Berg. The reference library is further down, below a gallery with administrative offices.

The entrance to the Cantonal Tribunal is in the southern part of the west wing. The large courtroom, which has a transverse, slightly raised new section, is decorated with a wall hanging by FERDINAND GEHR and his daughter FRANZISKA. The approach to the stairs has wall paintings by ALFRED KOBEL (b. 1925) of St.Gall.

The Abbey Archives of St.Gall, the property of both the Canton of St.Gall and the Catholic Church of the Canton, are kept in the western plinth storey and in the new building. They cover a period of more than twelve hundred years and guard the *legal documents (original deeds) and administrative records* of the former princely abbey of St.Gall, secularized in 1805. These records relate equally to ecclesiastical and to worldly matters. The oldest original documents go back to the first half of the 8th century. The collections of original private documents

186

and deeds of donation dating from the first millenium – amounting to some 700 – in which the donation of possessions to the Gallus Foundation is often legally described have almost no comparison with any other archival collection. There are also some *100 Carolingian and Ottonian parchments relating to sovereignty,* from before the turn of the millenium. A comparable collection of original private documents is to be found in the State Archives in Milan. The first documented archivist was Deacon Waldo in about 770. He was later abbot of St.Gall and Reichenau, then bishop of Basel and finally abbot of Saint-Denis in Paris, an important Carolingian personality with relations at the court of Charlemagne. The private documents, without seals, inform us about the social and political relations of Switzerland with Alsace, with southern Germany, and with the Vorarlberg in the last centuries of the first millenium of the Christian era. ⒩⒪⒫

100 Administrative building, north wing. Recently built atrium with ceiling paintings by Ferdinand Gehr.

187

Important manuscripts have also been kept in the Abbey Archives since time immemorial. Particularly noteworthy is the *St.Gall Memorial or Fraternity Book,* one of the seven books of this type preserved from the 10th century, in which the benefactors and brethren of the monastery are listed. The so-called *Professbuch,* dating from the early 9th century, can be claimed to be unique, as no other document of this type from the Carolingian epoch has come down to us. It records the profession of faith of the monks since Abbot Otmar, the founder of the monastery, as well as those of the 9th and 10th centuries, in contemporary script. In all, the Abbey Archives contain approximately 20,000 original documents, 3,000 manuscripts and several hundred fascicles of documents.

Also in the Foundation Archives are the *archives* of the former *princely abbey of Pfaefers,* secularized in 1838. They are the property of the Canton of St.Gall and comprise not only the archival records of the originally Rhaeto-Romanic monastery, but also a number of medieval manuscripts from its library. Of major importance is the *Carolingian Liber Viventium,* with full-page painted symbols of the evangelists. The *Liber Aureus* is a richly illuminated manuscript compendium of the late 14th and early 15th centuries; its name comes from the gilded clasps of its 16th-century binding. Finally, we should mention the so-called *Vidimus Heider,* a cartulary of 1590, with Renaissance miniatures and ornamentation.

The document collections of the former *abbey of St.Johann* in the Thurtal, which was incorporated into the monastery of St.Gall in 1555, are also in the Abbey Archives.

Like the canton itself, the *State Archives* were established in 1803. It was the first duty of the archivist to place in safety the *legal documents* necessary for administrative purposes that dated from the time of the old confederacy, before 1798, and the transition period from 1798 to 1803.

188

101 The eagle as symbol for John the Evangelist. Liber Viventium, about 800. From the Monastery of Pfaefers, now in the Abbey Archives.

189

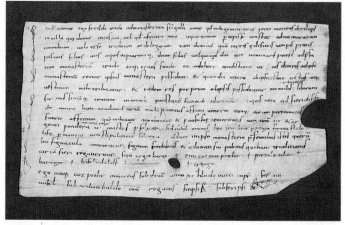

102 Carolingian deed of donation of 824, with first mention of Gossau, Canton of St.Gall. Abbey Archives.

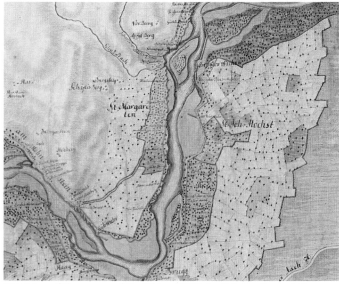

103 Map of the course of the Rhine, 1769, by Johann Conrad Roemer; detail from the bend of the Rhine at St.Margrethen. State Archives.

190

Before 1798 the area of the present canton consisted of a conglomerate of numerous regionally delimited administrative units. The most important rulers were the representatives of the old confederate localities and the prince-abbot of St.Gall. In addition, there were also the town-republics of St.Gall and Rapperswil.

The present archival collection largely documents these *complex relations* before the year 1800. For individual regions only partial collections have come down to us; important material remained with the old rulers, particularly in Zurich, and with the supervisory authority, the old Confederate Diet, the archives of which are in the State Archives of the Canton of Aargau. The administrative documents of the princely abbey of St.Gall are to be found in the Abbey Archives. A printed guide provides detailed information on the State Archives collections and on the history of the Archives.

After 1803, with the development of the administration, the State Archives took on their proper purpose: taking over, classifying, recording, safeguarding and conserving the documents worth preserving of the Great Council, the Administrative Council, the departments and their services and the courts and state institutions. In addition, collections which are of significance for the history of the canton are also placed in the State Archives for safekeeping.

The Cantonal Administration Library was established in 1845, the result of the merging of several decentralized departmental libraries. It existed as the State and Cantonal Library from 1889 to 1979, when the town library (Vadiana) was taken over by the Canton.

The Administration Library mainly houses *works on administrative law and the science of administration,* as well as St.Gall official publications and those relating to the history of the Canton of St.Gall in general. In addition, it is in charge of the automated library network of St.Gall.

The Children's or Guardian Angels Chapel

The planning for this chapel goes back to 1841/42, when there was an attempt to close the gap in the buildings between the Catholic School (today the Women's Vocational School), built in 1840 by FELIX WILHELM KUBLY and HANS CONRAD STADLER, and the arsenal wing, which had then been completed. Kubly's fourth project was carried out between 1843 and 1846. A first renovation took place in about 1900.

In 1970/71 the chapel was radically transformed under the direction of the architect HANS STADLIN of St.Gall. The exterior was largely restored to its original appearance and the interior greatly altered. The chapel occupies an *important position* at the entrance of the monastery area, where it provides the «hinge» to the transverse line of the Marktgasse, which enters the monastery square at this point.

The cube-shaped construction, horizontally divided by cornices at plinth height, in the centre and below the roof projection, turns towards the square a gabled entrance projection with a columned portico and a window with two lights, and has a flat hip-roof. The vertical divisions, of secondary importance, are provided by angle pilasters and closed round-arch windows which take in two stories. The interior is spanned by a cavetto vault and is divided by pilasters and blind arcades. The formerly U-shaped balcony on Tuscan columns has been reduced to the present organ loft. The triple triumphal arch of the projection contains a Biedermeier organ front. Of the former rich paintings, only the ceiling picture, «The Nativity» by ANTON BUETLER (1819–1874), remains. The liturgical furniture is modern. A crucifix and a statue of the Virgin Mary, both 17th century, are not part of the original fittings.

The Round Tower

The so-called round tower stands south of the new palace and is part of an approximately 40-metre section of the medieval *city fortifications,* originally crenellated, which still stand beween a new building of the 1950s and the *Charles Borromeo Gate.* They are visible from the outside. In fact, this tower is a semicircular masonry shell, irregularly shaped on the inside, covered by half of a conical roof. The masonry, consisting of large blocks, has been partially plastered and has some firing slits and flat-arch cannon embrasures. Gaol cells were built in the 17th century; they are no longer used today. The rooms on the upper floor, which were empty, are now used for storage. The *Gothic roof framework* is a circular construc-

104 The round tower with the city wall adjacent on the west side. The only remains of the medieval surround.

tion with steeply-angled foot- and head braces, perhaps dating back to the 14th century.

The ground floor below contains the *Staatskeller* (state cellar). The reception room of the Government was set up in 1953 on the occasion of the 150th anniversary of the Canton of St.Gall. It was a jubilee gift from the craftmen's association of St.Gall to the Council. The new open-beam ceiling with hefty cross timbers rests on two wooden pilasters. The walls are partly plastered. A painted map of the Canton of St.Gall depicts historical scenes. In addition, the artist WALTER VOGEL (b. 1899) decorated various sections of the ceiling with *heraldic paintings,* based on the armorial gallery in the Great Council Chamber. A total of 20 coats of arms of individual towns and old dominions of the area which now makes up the canton have been assembled in groups which belong together territorially, along with cantonal and confederacy coats of arms: the Town of St.Gall, Walenstadt, the Territory of Rheintal (bailiwick), Weesen, the County of Toggenburg, Oberberg (bailiwick), the Barony of Sax, Rheineck, Altstaetten, Sargans, Lichtensteig, Gams (bailiwick), the Old Territory of St.Gall, Wil, Rorschach, the County of Werdenberg, Sargans (bailiwick), the Territory of Gaster, Uznach and Rapperswil.

The Charles Borromeo Gate

In the Treaty of Rorschach of 1566 not only were the respective legal positions and property laws of the ecclesiastical precinct and the town established, but architectural measures were also decided upon. A partition wall, to be paid for by both parties, was to separate the monastic precinct from the rest of the town, and in return the abbot received permission to construct a gate in the southern part of the town wall at his own expense. This most recent of the eight former outer gates of the town is the only one which is still standing. It was built in 1569/70 by the master of works CASPAR GRAF, known as LINDENMANN. The marks of the stone cutters allow some of them to be identified by name: HANS OF BADEN, JAKOB, HANS and HEINRICH OF RORSCHACH, HEINRICH OF SCHWYZ, THOMAS OF REICHENHALL and ULRICH OF WELLHAUSEN near Constance. On 26 August 1570, on his journey through St.Gall, Cardinal Charles Borromeo is said to have been the first to pass through the gate, as is suggested by the fact that the gate acquired its name only subsequently.

The rectangular construction in rubble masonry with visible stone and a saddleback roof has a pointed-arch passageway and steps that allow access to Moosbruggstrasse, which lies at a lower level. After the dissolution of the monastery, the gate building was used as a gaol, the north windows and the roof section being altered for that purpose. In 1963/65 the building was restored on the outside and entirely reconstructed on the inside. Today it is used as the Cantonal Remand Prison. On the south side, framed by six rectangular windows with grilles, is a *monu-**mental sandstone relief,* in the form of a Renaissance edicula (shrine) crowned with Gothic ornamentation. In the lower section are the quartered monastic arms of Abbot Otmar Kunz (ruled 1564–1577): 1. The bear of the mon-

105 *Charles Borromeo Gate, sandstone relief with the arms of Abbot Otmar Kunz, by Baltus von Salmansweiler, 1570.*

astery of St.Gall; 2. The Lamb of God (monastery of St.Johann in the Thurtal, incorporated in 1555); 3. Serpent arms of Abbot Otmar Kunz, a native of Wil; 4. A mastiff (Toggenburg, belonging to St.Gall since 1468); above, mitre with crossed crosiers. In each corner is a putto. Next to them are figures in niches between pairs of Corinthian columns: left, a bearded Gallus as the hermit with the bear which, according to legend, helped him build his cell; right, Otmar in full abbot's regalia (he was the first abbot of the monastery), with a wine cask, referring to the miracle of the wine when the bones of the saint were transferred from the island of Werd at Stein am Rhein across Lake Constance in the year 769. Above, Christ hangs on a naturalistic Tree of the Cross, accompanied by the Sorrowing Virgin and St.John. At the foot of the cross, the skull of Adam recalls Golgotha. On the left are the arms of Pope Pius IV Medici (reigned 1559–1565), surmounted by a tiara and crossed keys; on the right are the crowned imperial arms with the double eagle, framed by the chain of the Order of the Golden Fleece. *The two coats of arms are rich in meaning.* The mark of respect to the Medici pope, who had died by 1570 and was the uncle of St.Charles Borromeo, relates to the fact that as early as 1565 Abbot Otmar had received spiritual jurisdiction from Rome, to the detriment of the Bishop of Constance. It was only in 1613 that the dispute with Constance was settled by a concordat. The imperial arms refer to the independence of the abbey of St.Gall from the empire and the ratification of the secular principality by Emperor Maximilian II (1564–1576). The two events are shown in two pictures of 1565, which are now in the Historical Museum in St.Gall.

At the foot of the relief stand two fettered lions facing each other, and below them squats a small man with a hammer and chisel, holding in front of himself a shield with stonecutter's marks and the letters B S. This is a self-portrait of the sculptor BALTUS VON SALMANSWEILER (Salem), dated 1570. The two side oculi with lion heads (the left one replaced) were originally perhaps masked firing slits. This Renaissance armorial relief, unique in Switzerland, would probably have been sacrificed to a «tidying up» programme, had not the politician and artist GEORG LEONHARD HARTMANN (1764–1828) of the town of St.Gall campaigned successfully in Aarau for its preservation.

Evangelical Reformed Church of St.Laurence

This church, which may have been established in the 9th century, originally stood *within the monastic enclosure* and was granted parochial rights before 1170. It was the centre of an extensive parish, which reached into Appenzell territory and into the principality; only in the Late Middle Ages does the church of St.Laurence seem to have become the church of the townspeople. After the city fire of 1418 a triple-nave basilica under a mighty saddleback roof was constructed under the architectural direction of MICHEL VON SAFOY of Salem. The gallery was enlarged northwards in 1513–1515, and southwards in 1577 by WOLFGANG VOEGELI. *The marked transformation* to a Neo-Gothic basilica took place in 1849–53 on the basis of plans by JOHANN GEORG MUELLER, which were successful against competing projects by JOHANN CHRISTOPH KUNKLER, FELIX WILHELM KUBLY and EMIL RITTMEYER. Kunkler was in charge of the construction work. The octagonal spire on the tower was designed by FERDINAND STADLER. For the total renovation of 1963–79 the restoration concept of JOHANN GEORG MUELLER was used. *The decorative painting* was carried out by the firm of HELBLING AND FONTANA of Jona, on the basis of a sketch by Mueller which had not been used previously. The architect was HANS-PETER NUESCH of St.Gall; the federal expert, ALBERT KNOEPFLI of Aadorf; IRMGARD GRUENINGER was in charge of the excavations.

The foundation walls of three previous churches lie below the northern part of the present church. The basilica with its nave and two aisles, enlarged by side aisles, has Gothic pillar arcades and ends in a rectangular choir.

106 St.Laurence. Late Gothic basic elements; Neo-Gothic transformation 1849/53 according to plans by Johann Georg Mueller. ▶

In the nave, a flat wood roof rests on broad arches; the side galleries have arcades and balustrades with tracery; the Neo-Gothic organcase is immense; the new organ is by the KUHN Company, 1979, and the stained glass of the choir by JULIUS GSELL, 1853. The marble baptismal front by KARL ULRICH RHEINER is of the same period. On the facade are the figures of the four evangelists, by JOHANN JAKOB OECHSLIN, copied by AUGUST RAUSCH.

The church building of St.Laurence allows us to follow the development of Historicism in Switzerland. On the one hand it is an attempt to preserve a monument, in the sense that the medieval church was not restored, but rather «completed»; on the other hand the close and oppressive church was «raised» to become a light basilica with a central nave elevated above the side aisles and its style adapted to the Gothic style of the Cathedral. The partially restored, partially original painting in the style of Italian inlay work has contributed to create one of the most significant church interiors of the 19th century.

107 St.Laurence. Main west entrance with two figures of Evangelists, by Johann Jakob Oechslin.

108 St.Laurence. Interior, looking east, painted 1978/79 on the basis of a decoration sketch of 1845 by Johann Georg Mueller.

A Selected Bibliography

ROBERT BAMERT, Zur Baugeschichte des Grossratssaales in der neuen Pfalz in St.Gallen, in: Unsere Kunstdenkmäler 32 (1981), pp. 147–158.
– Klosterhof und Pfalz der ehemaligen Fürstabtei St.Gallen (Manuscript).

HERMANN BAUER / PIUS RAST, Die Stiftskirche St.Gallen. Ein Bildband. St.Gallen 1967.

LINUS BIRCHLER, Stiftskirche und Stift Sankt Gallen. St.Gallen 1930 (Schweizer Kunstführer 6).

PAUL-HENRY BOERLIN, Die Stiftskirche St.Gallen. Ein Beitrag zur Geschichte der deutschen Barockarchitektur. Bern 1964.

JOHANNES DUFT, Die Glaubenssorge der Fürstäbte von St.Gallen im 17. und 18. Jahrhundert. Lucerne 1944.
– Sankt Gallus Gedenkbuch. St.Gall 1952.
– (Publisher) Studien zum St.Galler Klosterplan. Mitteilungen zur vaterländischen Geschichte 42. St.Gallen 1962, with contributions by Bernhard Bischoff, Johannes Duft, Heinrich Edelmann, P. Wolfgang Hafner, Walter Horn, P. Iso Müller, Erwin Poeschel and Hans Reinhart.
– Sankt Otmar in Kult und Kunst. Part I: Der Kult. Part II: Die Kunst. Neujahrsblatt des Historischen Vereins des Kantons St.Gallen 105 and 106 (1965 and 1966).
– Stiftsbibliothek Sankt Gallen. Geschichte – Barocksaal – Manuskripte. Uznach 1967.
– Die Gallus-Kapelle zu St.Gallen und ihr Bilderzyklus. Neujahrsblatt des Historischen Vereins 117 (1977; re-printed 1987).
– Die Stiftsbibliothek Sankt Gallen. St.Gall and Sigmaringen 1983 (3rd edition).
– Klosterbruder Gabriel Loser. Sein Anteil an den Barockbauten des Stiftes Sankt Gallen. St.Gall and Sigmaringen 1985.
– AND RUDOLF SCHNYDER, Die Elfenbein-Einbände der Stiftsbibliothek St.Gallen. Beuron 1984.
– AND ERNST ZIEGLER, St.Gallen. Kloster und Stadt. Bern 1984 (Schweizer Heimatbücher 187).

CHRISTOPH EGGENBERGER, Psalterium aureum Sancti Galli. Mittelalterliche Psalterillustration im Kloster St.Gallen. Sigmaringen 1987.

ADOLF FÄH, Die Kathedrale in St.Gallen. Bildmappe mit Text zur Baugeschichte. Zurich (ca. 1900).

ADOLF FÄH, Die Kathedrale in St.Gallen und die Stiftsbibliothek. Bild-
mappe, part II. Zurich (ca. 1900).
– Führer durch die Kathedrale von St.Gallen. Zurich 1913.
– Die Chorstühle der Kathedrale von St.Gallen. St.Gall 1923.
– Die Schicksale der Kathedrale von St.Gallen seit ihrer Erbauung.
Einsiedeln 1928.
– Die Stiftsbibliothek in St.Gallen. Der Bau und seine Schätze.
Neujahrsblatt des Historischen Vereins 69 (1929).
THEODOR GOHL, Restauration des Grossrathsaales in St.Gallen, in: Die
Eisenbahn 17 (1882), pp. 1–4.
JOSEF GRÜNENFELDER, Beiträge zum Bau der St.Galler Landkirchen
unter dem Offizialat P. Iso Walser 1759–1785. Schriften des Ver-
eins für Geschichte des Bodensees und seiner Umgebung 85
(1967), and separately.
– Stift St.Gallen. Langewische-Bücherei. Königstein im Taunus 1969.
– Das Blatt des Notker-Altars in der Kathedrale St.Gallen – Ein
Werk Martin Knollers? in: Unsere Kunstdenkmäler 34 (1983),
S. 199–204.
– and Albert Knoepfli, Kathedrale St.Gallen. Ehemalige Benedik-
tiner-Stiftskirche St.Gallus und Otmar. Schweizerischer Kunst-
führer. Basel 1967, 8th edition 1987.
HANS MARTIN GUBLER, Johann Caspar Bagnato und das Bauwesen des
Deutschen Ordens in der Ballei Elsass-Burgund im 18. Jahrhun-
dert. Sigmaringen 1985.
AUGUST HARDEGGER, Salomon Schlatter und Traugott Schiess. Die
Baudenkmäler der Stadt St.Gallen. St.Gall 1922.
– Die alte Stiftskirche und die ehemaligen Klostergebäude in
St.Gallen. Ein Rekonstruktionsversuch. Zurich 1917.
HELVETIA SACRA, part III: Die Orden mit Benediktinerregel, Vol. 1,
part 2, Bern 1986: St.Gallen, bearbeitet von Johannes Duft, An-
ton Gössi und Werner Vogler, pp. 1180–1369 (with an extensive
bibliography); also separately: Die Abtei St.Gallen. St.Gall and
Einsiedeln 1986.
P. RUDOLF HENGGELER, Professbuch der Fürstlichen Benediktinerab-
tei der Heiligen Gallus und Otmar zu St.Gallen. Zug 1929.
KATRIN S. ILBERTZ, Die acht Gallus-Reliefs in der Kathedrale von
St.Gallen von Johann Christian Wentzinger (1757–1759). Thesis,
Zurich 1985/86. Manuscript.
WALTER HORN AND ERNEST BORN, The Plan of St.Gall. A Study of the
Architecture and Economy of, and Life in, a Paradigmatic Carol-
ingian Monastery. 3 volumes. Berkley, Los Angeles and London
1979. Discussed in: Kunstchronik 35 (1982), pp. 89–96.
WERNER JACOBSEN, Ältere und neuere Forschungen um den St.Galler
Klosterplan, in: Unsere Kunstdenkmäler 34 (1983), pp. 134–151
(with extensive literature).

ALBERT KNOEPFLI, Kunstgeschichte des Bodenseeraums, Vol. 1: Von der Karolingerzeit bis zur Mitte des 14. Jahrhunderts. Bodensee-Bibliothek IV. Constance, Lindau and Stuttgart 1961.

– Die Kathedrale von St.Gallen und ihre Innenrestaurierung, in: Montfort 1966, pp. 156–185.

– Ein Wölbungsplan des 15. Jahrhunderts für den spätgotischen Hallenchor der Benediktiner-Stiftskirche St.Gallen, in: Schaffhauser Beiträge zur vaterländischen Geschichte 48 (1971), pp. 12–58, and separately.

– Und das nennen sie «Denkmalpflege» (zur Renovation der Jugendkirche), in: Unsere Kunstdenkmäler 22 (1971), pp. 44–47.

– St.Laurenzen und seine baulichen Schicksale, in: Die Kirche von St.Laurenzen in St.Gallen. St.Gall 1979.

EDWIN KOLLER, Eine neue Heimstätte für Staatsarchiv, Stiftsarchiv und Verwaltungsbibliothek, in: Der restaurierte Nordflügel des Regierungsgebäudes in St.Gallen. St.Gall 1979.

INGEBORG KRUMMER-SCHROTH, Christian Wentzinger. Bildhauer, Maler, Architekt, 1710–1797. Freiburg i. Br. 1987.

KUNSTFÜHRER DURCH DIE SCHWEIZ. Bern 1975 (6th edition).

WALTER LENDI AND ELENA ENG, St.Galler Stadtführer. St.Gall 1975.

DIETER MEILE, Kunstgeschichtliche und städtebauliche Würdigung, in: Der restaurierte Nordflügel des Regierungsgebäudes in St.Gallen. St.Gall 1979.

J. LUDWIG MEYER, der ehemalige Kapitelsaal und die neue Pfalz des Stiftes St.Gallen, in: Anzeiger für Schweizerische Alterthumskunde 16 (1883), pp. 379–381.

ERWIN POESCHEL, Die Kunstdenkmäler des Kantons St.Gallen, vol. II. Die Stadt St.Gallen: part 1; vol. III. Die Stadt St.Gallen: part 2. Das Stift. Basel 1957 and 1961.

ADOLF REINLE, Die entscheidenden Vorprojekte der barocken St.Galler Stiftskirche, in: Zeitschrift für Schweizerische Archäologie und Kunstgeschichte 24 (1965/66), pp. 1–15.

HANS REINHARDT, Der St.Galler Klosterplan. St.Gall 1962.

MICHEL REISTLE, Josef Wannenmacher (1722–1780). Manuscript (in print).

DORA FANNY RITTMEYER, Die Goldschmiedekunst der Kathedrale in St.Gallen. Neujahrsblatt des Historischen Vereins 71 (1931).

PETER ROELLIN, St.Gallen. Stadtveränderung und Stadterlebnis im 19. Jahrhundert. St.Gall 1981.

BEAT MATTHIAS VON SCARPATETTI, Die Handschriften der Stiftsbibliothek St.Gallen, Codices 1726–1984. St.Gall 1983.

ALOIS SCHEIWILLER, Das Kloster St.Gallen. Einsiedeln, Köln and St.Gall 1937.

GUSTAV SCHERRER, Verzeichnis der Handschriften der Stiftsbibliothek von St.Gallen. Halle 1875.

BENNO SCHUBIGER, Die Vollendung des St.Galler Klosterplatzes im 19. Jahrhundert. Die Planungen und Bauten von Hans Conrad Stadler und Felix Wilhelm Kubly, in: Zeitschrift für Schweizerische Archäologie und Kunstgeschichte 37 (1980), pp. 123–144.
  – Die barocke Schutzengelrotunde im St.Galler Klosterhof, in: Unsere Kunstdenkmäler 34 (1983), pp. 205–211.
  – Felix Wilhelm Kubly (1802–1872). Ein Schweizer Architekt zwischen Klassizismus und Historismus. St.Galler Kultur und Geschichte 13 (1984).
HANS RUDOLF SENNHAUSER, Das Münster des Abtes Gozbert (816–837) und seine Ausmalung unter Hartmut (Proabbas 841, Abt 872–883), in: Unsere Kunstdenkmäler 34 (1983), pp. 152–167.
  – Das Lapidarium in St.Gallen. Kommentar zu den Ausstellungsstücken. Manuscript and recording.
WERNER VOGLER AND HANS MARTIN GUBLER, Der St.Galler Stiftsbezirk in den Plänen von P. Gabriel Hecht 1720–1726: Text- und Bildband. Rorschach 1986.
  – Das Hochaltarbild der St.Galler Stiftskirche, in: Zeitschrift für Schweizerische Archäologie und Kunstgeschichte 36 (1979), pp. 248–258.
FRANZ WEIDMANN, Geschichte der Stifts-Bibliothek. St.Gall 1841.

The Artists
(a selection)

PIETRO ANDREOTA. Architect from Roveredo in Mesocco. Rebuilt the Otmar Church (1623–28), monastery buildings in Neu St.Johann (1626–30).

EGID QUIRIN ASAM (1692–1750). Together with his brother, Cosmas Damian, chief master of Munich Baroque. Probably identical with the «Munich stucco artist» who in 1730 decorated the festival hall (today the bishop's residence).

JOHANN CASPAR BAGNATO (1696–1757). Architect from Como. Architectural consultant for the Deutschordensgesellschaft. Basic plan for the abbey church (1750), Kornhaus Rorschach (1746/47), Rathaus Bischofszell and numerous buildings in south Germany.

GIULIO BARBIERI. Architect from Roveredo in Mesocco. Project for the palace wing (1666/67) and reconstruction of the monastery of Pfäfers (1670/71) (together with Giovanni Serro); also worked on the monastery church of Isny.

JOHANN MICHAEL BEER (1696–1780). Architect from Au in the Bregenzerwald. Supervision of the construction of the choir and of the two towers of the abbey church. Further works included the parish churches of Kirchberg and Niederbüren (both St.Gall) as well as the chapel of the castle of Mammern (Thurgau).

JOHANN FERDINAND BEER (1731–1789). Architect from Au in the Bregenzerwald. New Palace (1767–69), numerous St.Gall parish churches, including St.Fiden, Bernhardzell, Kirchberg and Wildhaus.

ANDREAS BENTELE. Stucco artist from Hangnach near Lindau. Stucco decoration in the dining room (1752/53), altars in Lindau, Bregenz and Kirchberg (St.Gall).

JOSEF BÜSSER (1896–1952). Sculptor from Bütschwil (St.Gall). Reliefs in the southwest entrance hall of the cathedral (1935), numerous works in St.Gall churches.

ANTONI DICK (d. 1785). Painter from Isny, died in St.Fiden (St.Gall). Restoration of the paintings of the cupola (1773), ceiling paintings in St.Fiden, Häggenschwil and Waldkirch.

FRANZ ANTON DIRR (1724–1801). Sculptor and altar builder, brother of Johann Georg, born in Weilheim (Bavaria), resided in Überlingen. Design for the choir screen (1771), bronze reliefs for the rotunda altars (1772) and chancel (1786), altars in St.Fiden, Berg and Mühlrüti (all St.Gall).

JOHANN GEORG DIRR (1723–1779). Stucco artist and sculptor, brother of Franz Anton, resided in Mimmenhausen. Worked with Feuchtmayer in the production of the confessionals and the choir stalls (1761–69), stucco decorations in the prelate's residence of the monastery of Salem.

HANS JÖRG DÖRIG. Altar builder from Wil (St.Gall). Former high altar in the abbey church and further appointments in the Otmar Church (1623 and sub.); furniture in the upper sacristy, monastery of Neu St.Johann (1628/29).

JOSEF ANTON FEUCHTMAYER (1696–1770). Sculptor and stucco artist from Wessobrunn. One of the chief exponents of Bavarian Rococo. Choir stalls in the abbey church, further major works in Birnau, Salem and Weingarten.

JOHANN GEORG and MATHIAS GIGL. Stucco artists from Wessobrunn, brothers. Stucco decorations in the abbey church and in the Library. Further works in Kirchberg (St.Gall), Ittingen and Isny.

DANIEL GLATTBURGER. Chief architect in St.Gall, palace wing (execution) and buildings within the monastery enclosure (1667 and sub.). Probably completed the monastery church of Neu St.Johann (1678–80), vaulting of the central nave of the minster in Constance (1679).

THEODOR GOHL (1844–1910). Cantonal architect 1880–91, born in Aarberg. Previously municipal architect in Winterthur; after 1892, deputy departmental head for architecture in the Confederacy. Reconstruction of the Great Council Chamber (1881/82), construction of the psychiatric clinic in Wil (St.Gall) (from 1884 on), the Technikum Winterthur and main post office in Zug.

HANS HAGGENBERG (d. after 1515). Painter and book illustrator from Winterthur. In the service of Abbot Ulrich Rösch (1463–1491) and Bishop Hugo von Hohenlandenberg (1496–1532). Paintings in the Gothic choir of the abbey church (about 1490), works preserved in Rorschach-Mariaberg and in Wil (St.Gall), as well as in many churches in the canton of Zurich.

GABRIEL HECHT (1664–1745). Member of the monastery of St.Gall, amateur architect and draftsman from Wangen in Allgäu. Plans for the arrangement of the monastery and reconstruction and restoration projects (1720–26). Conceived the emblematic pictures in the dean's wing.

JOHANN SEBASTIAN HERSCHE (1619 – after 1691). Court painter of the abbot of St.Gall, born in Appenzell, resided in St.Fiden. Pictures in the Gallus and palace chapels (about 1670), works throughout East Switzerland.

JOSEF KELLER (1740–1823). Painter from Pfronten in Allgäu, later resident in Zug. Painting of the apse of the abbey church (1815), ceiling paintings in Wittenbach (St.Gall) (1812); otherwise active principally in Central Switzerland.

DANIEL FRIEDRICH KIRCHHOFER (1831–1855). Embroidery designer in St.Gall. Painting of the Great Council Chamber in the Palace (1881).

FELIX WILHELM KUBLY (1802–1872). Architect from Altstätten, residing in St.Gall since 1835. Exponent of Munich Historicism. Zeughaus wing and Kinderkapelle (1838-46), renovation project for St.Laurence (1846), Kantonsschule St.Gall (1856), churches in Heiden and Wattwil. Extensive production.

JOHANN CHRISTOPH KUNKLER (1813–1898). Architect in St.Gall. Projects for St.Laurence (1846), Altes Museum (1873–77) and Bürgerspital (1841–45) in St.Gall, reformed churches in Rapperswil and Niederuzwil (St.Gall). Bad and Trinkhalle in Bad Ragaz.

CASPAR LINDENMANN. Architect from Rorschach, bore the family name Graf. Charles Borromeo Gate and Bruderhaus (about 1570). Crown of tower of Radolfzell Church (1576/77).

GABRIEL LOSER (1701–1785). Brother in the monastery of St.Gall. Sculptor and cabinet maker, born in Wasserburg at Lake Constance. Model of the abbey church (1751/1752); head of the monastery workshop. Main personage involved in the Library decorations.

ALFONS MAGG (1891–?). Sculptor in Zurich. Restorer and copier of the sandstone figures on the abbey church (from 1920 on); extensive production.

CASPAR MOOSBRUGGER (1656–1723). Monastery member in Einsiedeln, architect from Au in the Bregenzerwald. Designs for a new church and monastery arrangement (1720/21). Built the monastery church of Einsiedeln. Consultant for almost all important monastery buildings in Switzerland.

JOHANN GEORG MÜLLER (1822–1849). Architect from Mosnang, resided in Wil (St.Gall). Introduced Historicism into Switzerland. Project for St.Laurence (1845). Design for the cathedral facade in Florence (1843), Altlerchenfeldkirche in Vienna (1849–51).

JOHANN JAKOB OECHSLIN (1820–1873). Sculptor from Schaffhausen. Sandstone statues in front of the Gallus Chapel (1842) and on the facade of St.Laurence (1854). Important exponent of Historicism.

JOSEF ANTON PULLACHER (1737–1799). Painter from Telfs in the Tyrol. Painted the former Throne Room in the New Palace (1786); paintings in the church in Niederhelfenschwil (St.Gall) (1787). Principally active in the Tyrol.

JOHANN JAKOB RISCHER (1662–1755). Architect from Schwarzenberg (?) in the Bregenzerwald. Project for restoration of the abbey church (1754); principally active in Mannheim and Heidelberg.

JOHANN RUEFF (1686–1750). Architect from Au in the Bregenzerwald. Project for St.Gall (1749/50); active in the wake of Br. Caspar Moosbrugger, *inter alia* in Einsiedeln and Engelberg.

MICHEL VON SAFOY. Architect from Salem, belonged to a newcomer family from Savoy. St.Laurence in St.Gall (1413–23).

BALTUS VON SALMANSWEILER. Sculptor from Salem. Creator of the relief on the Charles Borromeo Gate (1570), where he represented himself.

HANS SCHENCK. Sculptor from Constance. Altar figures in the Otmar Church (1623/24) and on the High Altar in Neu St.Johann (1641).

DAVID ALOIS SCHMID (1791–1861). Landscape painter and draftsman from Schwyz. Paintings in the so-called relief room in the New Palace (1850). Tender portraitist of the Swiss landscape.

GIOVANNI SERRO. Architect from Roveredo in Mesocco. Author of the project for the Palace wing in St.Gall (1666/67) and for the monastery of Pfäfers (1670/71) (together with Giulio Barbieri). Abbey church of Kempten (Kuppel) and further churches in Bavaria.

FIDEL SPORER. Sculptor and stucco artist from Weingarten. Student of Christian Wenzinger. Pew balusters (1757) and stucco altars below the cupola (1772). Statues in the reading room of the library in Schussenried.

HANS CONRAD STADLER (1788-1846). Architect in Zurich. Exponent of Late Classicism, student of Weinbrenner in Karlsruhe. Gallusstrasse 16 (1826), project for the north wing of the monastery square (1830), Catholic School next to the Children's Chapel (1838/39) (together with Kubly).

FERDINAND STADLER (1813–1870). Architect of Zurich, important exponent of Historicism. Project and execution for the tower of St.Laurence (1850/51), synagogue in Lengnau (1845/46), Elizabethenkirche in Basel (1857–65), Glarus Church (1864–66).

PETER THUMB (1681–1766). Architect from Bezau in the Bregenzerwald, nave and rotunda of the abbey church (1755–60) and Library (1758–69); Church of Lachen (Schwyz). Pilgrimage Church of Birnau, monastery of St.Peter in Schwarzwald, Schwarzach etc.

WOLFGANG VÖGELI (d. 1586). Municipal master of works in St.Gall, born in Lenzburg (Aargau), became resident in 1547. St.Laurence (south side nave), St.Mangen (tower), Waaghaus, Sailer Mädchenschule (today Kugelgasse 19).

JOSEF WANNENMACHER (1722–1780). Painter from Tomerdingen (Württemberg). Painted the entire abbey church (nave under the direction of Christian Wenzinger) and the Library; Pilgrimage Church of Deggingen, Dominican church of Rottweil, Franciscan church of Schwäbisch-Gmünd etc.

CHRISTIAN WENZINGER (1710–1797). Sculptor, painter and architect from Freiburg im Breisgau, one of the principal exponents of the South-German Late Baroque. General superintendent for the artistic appointments in the nave rotunda of the abbey church; personally decorated the figures (1757–61).

The Abbots of the Monastery of St.Gall

719–759	Otmar
759/60–782	Johannes
782	Ratpert
782–784	Waldo
784–812	Werdo
812–816	Wolfleoz
816–837	Gozbert
837–840/41	Bernwig
840/841	Engilbert
841–872	Grimald
872–883	Hartmut
883–890	Bernhard
890–919	Salomon
922–925	Hartmann
925–933	Engilbert
933–942	Thieto
942–958	Craloh Anno, anti-abbot 953–954
958–971	Purchart (I)
971–975	Notker
976–984	Ymmo
984–990	Ulrich (I)
990–1001	Kerhart
1001–1022	Purchart (II)
1022–1034	Thietpald
1034–1072	Nortbert
1072–1076	Ulrich (II)
1077–1121	Ulrich von Eppenstein Lutold, anti-abbot 1077 – ca. 1083 Werinhar, anti-abbot 1083–1086
1121–1133	Manegold von Mammern Heinrich von Twiel, anti-abbot 1121–22
1133–1167	Werinher

1167–1199	Ulrich von Tegerfeld
1199–1200	Ulrich von Veringen
1200–1204	Heinrich von Klingen
1204–1220	Ulrich von Sax
1220–1226	Rudolf von Güttingen
1226–1239	Konrad von Bussnang
1239–1244	Walter von Trauchburg
1244–1272	Berchtold von Falkenstein
1272–1277	Ulrich von Guettingen Heinrich von War- tenberg, anti-abbot 1272–1274
1277–1281	Rumo von Ramstein, anti- abbot 1274–1277)
1281–1301	Wilhelm von Montfort Konrad von Gundel- fingen, anti-abbot 1288–1291
1301–1318	Heinrich von Ramstein
1318–1329	Hiltbold von Werstein Rudolf von Montfort, curator 1330–1333
1333–1360	Hermann von Bonstetten
1360–1379	Georg von Wildenstein
1379–1411	Kuno von Stoffeln

1411–1418	Heinrich von Gundelfingen
1418–1419	Konrad von Pegau
1419–1426	Heinrich von Mansdorf
1426–1442	Eglolf Blarer
1442–1457	Kaspar von Breitenlandenberg († 1463)
1463–1491	Ulrich Rösch (curator 1457–1463)
1491–1504	Gotthard Giel von Glattburg
1504–1529	Franz Gaisberg
1529–1530	Kilian Germann
1530–1564	Diethelm Blarer von Wartensee
1564–1577	Otmar Kunz
1577–1594	Joachim Opser
1594–1630	Bernhard Mueller
1630–1654	Pius Reher
1654–1687	Gallus Alt
1687–1696	Coelestin Sfondrati
1696–1717	Leodegar Bürgisser
1717–1740	Joseph von Rudolphi
1740–1767	Coelestin Gugger von Staudach
1767–1796	Beda Angehrn
1796–1805	Pankraz Vorster († 1829)

Prince-Abbot Coelestin Gugger von Staudach (ruled 1740–1767)

Prince-Abbot Pankraz Vorster (ruled 1796–1805), † 1829

Azure two walking sticks in saltire handles in chief or

Ulrich Rösch
1463–1491

Chequi gules and argent a chief argent

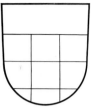

Gotthard Giel
1491–1504

Or a he goat rampant sable

Franz Gaisberg
1504–1529

Or a unicorn rampant azure

Kilian Germann
1529–1530

Argent a cock langued and its dexter leg raised gules armed or its comb and wattles charged with a cross couped or

Diethelm Blarer von Wartensee
1530–1564

Azure between three mounts vert issuing in base and a mullet of six points in chief or a serpent gliding to the dexter its head erect and body wavy or

Otmar Kunz
1564–1577

Azure statant on the centre one of three mounts issuing in base vert a dove argent holding in its beak by the stalk a leaf vert

Joachim Opser
1577–1594

Or a millwheel its spokes in saltire issuing from a mascle sable surmounted by an arrow palewise point downwards argent flighted gules

Bernhard Müller
1594–1630

212

Gules three bendlets sinister argent between two flowers of eight petals or slipped and each with two leaves bendwise sinister vert

Pius Reher
1630–1654

Argent a cock its dexter leg raised sable combed wattled and holding in its beak gules by the stalk a bunch of grapes azure stalked and leaved vert

Gallus Alt
1654–1687

Gluarterly 1 and 4 azure a bend wavy or charged with a bend azure between two mullets of six points or: 2 and 3 argent a tree palewise eradicated vert

Coelestin Sfondrati
1687–1696

Azure on three mounts issuing in base vert a double towered castle argent its base roof and battlements gules

Leodegar Bürgisser
1696–1717

Or a demi ram sable

Joseph von Rudolfi
1717–1740

Quarterly 1 and 4 or three mounts issuing in base vert thereon a fence of five pales surmounting a bar gules statant on the centre pale a cuckoo holding suspended beneath its beak an egg both proper: 2 and 3 azure issuing from the base a sprig of rose with four leaves vert and three flowers one and two gules seeded or

Coelestin Gugger von Staudach
1740–1767

Azure between two wings or a pile reversed argent charged with a fir tree issuing palewise vert from the centre of three mounts issuant in base also vert on a chief azure three mullets of six points or

Beda Angehrn
1767–1796

Vert a demi bear couped argent langued and armed gules

Pankraz Vorster
1796–1805

213

The Bishops of the Diocese of St.Gall

1805–1823 Apostolic vicar-generalship, still under Constance

1823–1833 Double bishopric Chur-St.Gall under bishop Karl Rudolf von Schauenstein

1834–1836 Non-acceptance of the double bishopric by the cantonal administration under bishop Johann Georg Bossi of Chur

1836–1847 Vicar-general Johann Peter Mirer

1847–1862 Johann Peter Mirer von Obersaxen, first bishop of St.Gall

1862–1882 Karl Johann Greith von Rapperswil

1882–1906 Augustin Egger von Kirchberg

1906–1913 Ferdinand Rüegg von St.Gallenkappel

1913–1930 Robert Bürkler von Alt St.Johann

1930–1938 Alois Scheiwiler von Waldkirch

1938–1957 Joseph Meile von Mosnang

1957–1976 Joseph Hasler von Altstätten († 1985)

1976– Otmar Mäder von Mörschwil

*Johann Peter Mirer
von Obersaxen,
first bishop of St.Gall (1847–1862)*

*Karl Johann Greith
von Rapperswil,
second bishop of St.Gall
(1862–1882)*

The Cantonal Presidents of the Canton of St.Gall

From 23 February 1815
to 30 June 1831
(change on 1st July)

1815/16 Karl Müller
von Friedberg
1816/17 Hieronymus Zollikofer
1817/18 Karl Müller
von Friedberg
1818/19 Hieronymus Zollikofer
1819/20 Karl Müller
von Friedberg
1820/21 Hieronymus Zollikofer
1821/22 Karl Müller
von Friedberg

1822/23 Hieronymus Zollikofer
1823/24 Karl Müller
von Friedberg
1824/25 Hieronymus Zollikofer
1825/26 Karl Müller
von Friedberg
1826/27 Hieronymus Zollikofer
1827/28 Karl Müller
von Friedberg
1828/29 Hieronymus Zollikofer
(†) and
Hermann von Fels
1829/30 Karl Müller
von Friedberg
1830/31 Hermann von Fels

Karl Müller von Friedberg (1755–1836) of Näfels, Founder of the canton of St.Gall, 1803. First Cantonal president.

Gallus Jakob Baumgartner (1797–1869) of Altstätten, Cantonal president and political commentator.

215

1831 (2) Hermann von Fels
1832 Gallus Jakob Baumgartner /
Johannes Stadler
1833 Joachim Pankraz Reutti /
Gallus Jakob Baumgartner
1834 Johannes Stadler /
Wilhelm Näff
1835 Gallus Jakob Baumgartner /
Johannes Stadler
1836 Wilhelm Näff /
Gallus Jakob Baumgartner
1837 Johannes Stadler /
Wilhelm Näff
1838 Gallus Jakob Baumgartner /
Johannes Stadler
1839 Wilhelm Näff /
Gallus Jakob Baumgartner
1840 Johannes Stadler /
Friedrich Fels
1841 Gallus Jakob Baumgartner /
Johannes Stadler
1842 Wilhelm Näff /
Friedrich Fels
1843 Johannes Stadler /
Gallus Jakob Baumgartner
1844 Friedrich Fels /
Wilhelm Näff
1845 Johannes Stadler /
Basil Ferdinand Curti
1846 Gallus Jakob Baumgartner /
Wilhelm Näff
1847 Johannes Stadler /
Matthias Hungerbühler
1848 Wilhelm Näff /
Johannes Stadler
1849 Basil Ferdinand Curti /
Johann Baptist Weder
1850 Friedrich Fels /
Matthias Hungerbühler
1851 Peter Steiger /
Felix Helbling
1852 Matthias Hungerbühler /
Peter Steiger
1853 Basil Ferdinand Curti /
Matthias Hungerbühler
1854 Felix Helbling /
Peter Steiger
1855 Basil Ferdinand Curti /
Felix Helbling
1856 Matthias Hungerbühler /
Otto Aepli
1857 Joseph Marzell Hoffmann /
Peter Steiger
1858 Matthias Hungerbühler /
Basil Ferdinand Curti
1859 Peter Steiger /
Gallus Jakob Baumgartner
1860 Anton Höfliger /
Peter Steiger
1861 Gallus Jakob Baumgartner /
Otto Aepli
1862 Johann Baptist Weder /
Otto Aepli
1863 Matthias Hungerbühler /
Gallus Jakob Baumgartner
1864 Otto Aepli / Georg Sailer
1865 Georg Sailer / Otto Aepli
1866 Johann Baptist Müller /
Eduard Steiger
1867 Joseph Marzell Hoffmann /
Georg Sailer
1868 Adolf Saxer /
Johann Zünd
1869 Georg Sailer / Otto Aepli
1870 Adolf Saxer / Georg Sailer
1871 Otto Aepli / Johann Zünd
1872 Sigismund Zäch /
Friedrich von Tschudi
1873 Flavian Bislin /
Matthias Hungerbühler
1874 Hermann Seifert /
Sigismund Zäch
1875 Kaspar Pfändler /
Johann Josef Keel
1876 Ludwig Zollikofer /
Matthias Hungerbühler

1877	Friedrich von Tschudi / Ferdinand Curti
1878	Matthias Hungerbühler / Otto Thuli
1879	Thomas Thoma / Ludwig Zollikofer
1880	Friedrich von Tschudi / Kaspar Pfändler
1881	Johann Josef Keel / Thomas Thoma
1882	Ferdinand Curti / Ludwig Zollikofer
1883	Kaspar Pfändler / Johann Josef Keel
1884	Thomas Thoma / Otto Thuli
1885	Ferdinand Curti / Ludwig Zollikofer
1886	Johann Josef Keel / Adolf Fehr
1887	Ferdinand Curti / Kaspar Pfändler
1888	Johannes Segmüller / Ludwig Zollikofer
1889	Ferdinand Curti / Thomas Thoma
1890	Kaspar Pfändler / Johann Josef Keel
1891	Ferdinand Curti

From 1st July 1891 on
(change on 1st July)

1891/92	Ludwig Zollikofer
1892/93	Johann Josef Keel
1893/94	Josef Scherrer-Füllemann
1894/95	Eduard Scherrer
1895/96	Johann Schubiger
1896/97	Adolf Kaiser
1897/98	Ludwig Zollikofer
1898/99	Johann Baptist Rukstuhl
1899/1900	Theodor Curti
1900/01	Eduard Scherrer
1901/02	Johann Schubiger
1902/03	Adolf Kaiser
1903/04	Ludwig Zollikofer
1904/05	Johann Baptist Rukstuhl
1905/06	Albert Mächler
1906/07	Heinrich Scherrer
1907/08	Anton Messmer
1908/09	Alfred Riegg
1909/10	Adolf Kaiser
1910/11	Edwin Rukstuhl
1911/12	Albert Mächler
1912/13	Heinrich Scherrer
1913/14	Johann Schubiger
1914/15	Alfred Riegg
1915/16	Johann Hauser
1916/17	Gottlieb Baumgartner
1917/18	Edwin Rukstuhl
1918/19	Albert Mächler
1919/20	Heinrich Scherrer
1920/21	Alfred Riegg
1921/22	Edwin Rukstuhl
1922/23	Otto Weber
1923/24	Gottlieb Baumgartner
1924/25	Emil Mäder
1925/26	Albert Mächler
1926/27	Emil Grünenfelder
1927/28	Alfred Riegg
1928/29	Edwin Rukstuhl
1929/30	Gottlieb Baumgartner
1930/31	Emil Mäder
1931/32	Albert Mächler
1932/33	Emil Grünenfelder
1933/34	Valentin Keel
1934/35	Gottlieb Baumgartner
1935/36	Edwin Rukstuhl

217

1936/37	Karl Kobelt	1963/64	Gottfried Hoby
1937/38	Emil Grünenfelder	1964/65	Guido Eigenmann
1938/39	Valentin Keel	1965/66	Albert Scherrer
1939/40	Adolf Roemer	1966/67	Simon Frick
1940/41	Josef Riedener	1967/68	Edwin Koller
1941/42	Joh. Jak. Gabathuler	1968/69	Mathias Eggenberger
1942/43	Albert Gemperli	1969/70	Hans Schneider
1943/44	Ernst Graf	1970/71	Gottfried Hoby
1944/45	Josef Riedener	1971/72	Willy Herrmann
1945/46	Adolf Roemer	1972/73	August Schmuki
1946/47	Alfred Kessler	1973/74	Willi Geiger
1947/48	Paul Müller	1974/75	Edwin Koller
1948/49	Joh. Jak. Gabathuler	1975/76	Florian Schlegel
1949/50	Albert Gemperli	1976/77	Ernst Rüesch
1950/51	Adolf Roemer	1977/78	Gottfried Hoby
1951/52	Josef Riedener	1978/79	Willy Herrmann
1952/53	Simon Frick	1979/80	Edwin Koller
1953/54	Paul Müller	1980/81	Willi Geiger
1954/55	Mathias Eggenberger	1981/82	Paul Gemperli
1955/56	Walter Clavadetscher	1982/83	Florian Schlegel
1956/57	Albert Gemperli	1983/84	Ernst Rüesch
1957/58	Adolf Roemer	1984/85	Karl Mätzler
1958/59	Josef Riedener	1985/86	Willi Geiger
1959/60	Simon Frick	1986/87	Edwin Koller
1960/61	Paul Müller	1987/88	Burkhard Vetsch
1961/62	Mathias Eggenberger	1988/89	Paul Gemperli
1962/63	Hans Schneider	1989/90	Hans Rohrer

Index

220

God the Father 67
Gods, see mythology
Gohl, Theodore, cantonal builder 165
Gossau 76
Gozbert, abbot 11, 15, 120, 123, 124, 126 (illustr.)
Graf, Caspar, known as Lindenmann, master builder 18, 195
Gregory the Great, pope and Father of the Church 62, 78, 80, 104, 105
Gregory of Nazianzus, patriarch 79 (illustr.), 80, 100, 108
Greith, Karl, bishop 155
Griffenberg, Heinrich, master builder 17
Grimald, abbot 119
Gronovius, Jacobus, publisher 115
Gruebler, Pankranz, baron 183
Grueninger, Irmgard, archeologist 198
Gsell, Julius, glass painter 200
Gugger von Staudach, abbot 12, 22, 24, 28 (illustr.), 31, 45, 46, 53, 60, 69, 84, 85, 86, 181 (illustr.)
Gunzo, Alemann, duke 147
Gutwein, Johann Wilhelm, goldsmith 56

Haedener, Johann, engraver 23 (illustr.)
Haggenberg, Hans, painter 17, 122
Haggenmueller, Hans Joerg, stucco artist 154
Hailand, F. Chrysostomus 56
Haenny, Ulrich, painter 159
Harsch, F. Maurus 128
Hartker, monk and recluse 154
Haertli, Caspar, illuminator 122
Hartmann, Georg Leonhard, artist 197
Hartmut, abbot 119

Hasler, Josephus, bishop 62
Haug, F. Karl 56
Hecht, F. Gabriel, architect 19 (illustr.), 20 (illustr.), 22, 57 (illustr.), 58, 84, 123, 137
– Xaver, painter 43
Heinrich II, St. 72
Heito, abbot of Reichenau 15
Helbling and Fontana 198
Henner, F. Hieronymus 128
Herkomer, Johann Georg, goldsmith 56
Hermann the Lame (Contractus), monk 63, 152
Herovits, Johann, restorer 166
Herrmann, Franz Ludwig, painter 156
Hersche, Johann, Sebastian, painter 144 (illustr.), 145, 151
Herter von Hertler, F. Innozenz 56
Hiacynthus, catacomb saint 76
Hiltibold, deacon 146
Hippocrates, Greek physician 112
Holbein, Hans the Younger, painter 94
Holy Ghost 62, 100, 101 (illustr.), 102, 107
Honoratus, catacomb saint 76

Idda, St. 72, 138
Ignatius Loyola, St. 71
– Theophorus, St. 75
Ildefonds of Toledo, St. 62
Immenot, F. Blasius 56
Isenring, Johann Baptist, engraver 25 (illustr.), 165

Jahveh 80
James the Elder, St. 82
– the Younger, St. 82
Jansen, Br. Mathias 60, 69, 81
Jerome, Father of the Church 80, 106, 127, 130 (illustr.)
Joachim, St. 67

224

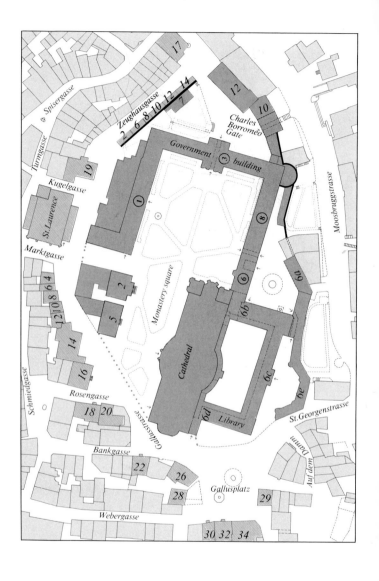